The Resurrection
of Jesus Christ

WITHDRAWN
FROM STOCK

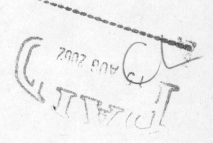

The Resurrection of Jesus Christ

Edited by
Paul Avis

DARTON·LONGMAN + TODD

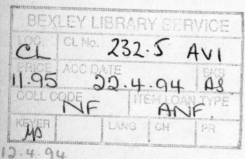

BEXLEY LIBRARY SERVICE

LOC	CL No.		
CL	232·5 AVI		
PRICE	ACC DATE		BKS
11·95	22.4.94		A8
COLL CODE		ITEM LOAN TYPE	
NF		ANF	
KEYER		LANG	CH	PR
MB				

12·4·94

First published in 1993 by
Darton, Longman and Todd Ltd
1 Spencer Court, 140–142 Wandsworth High Street
London SW18 4JJ

This collection © 1993 Paul Avis

ISBN 0–232–52047–X

A catalogue record for this book is available
from the British Library

Cover: *The Resurrection* by El Greco, Prado, Madrid/Bridgeman
Art Library, London; design by Pat Craddock.

Typeset by Intype, London SW19 8DR
Printed and bound in Great Britain
at Page Bros, Norwich

Contents

1 The Resurrection of Jesus: Asking the Right   1
 Questions
 Paul Avis

2 The Meaning of the Resurrection of Jesus   23
 Paul Badham

3 The Four Gospels: Four Perspectives on the   39
 Resurrection
 John Fenton

4 The Resurrection: History, Story and Belief   50
 Leslie Houlden

5 Interpreting the Resurrection   68
 Christopher Rowland

6 Is the Resurrection a 'Historical' Event? Some   85
 Muddles and Mysteries
 Sarah Coakley

7 The Resurrection and the Empty Tomb   116
 Barnabas Lindars, SSF

8 God who raises the Dead: The Resurrection of   136
 Jesus and Early Christian Faith in God
 Richard Bauckham

9 The Resurrection and the Incarnation   155
 Brian Hebblethwaite

10 Resurrection and Rationality   171
 Adrian Thatcher

Notes on contributors

Paul Avis is Vicar of Stoke Canon and Prebendary of Exeter and a member of the Church of England General Synod and Doctrine Commission.

Paul Badham is Professor of Theology and Dean of the Faculty of Theology, St David's University College, Lampeter.

John Fenton is Canon Emeritus, Christ Church, Oxford.

Leslie Houlden is Professor of Christian Theology, King's College, London.

Christopher Rowland is Dean Ireland's Professor, Queen's College, Oxford.

Sarah Coakley is Professor of Christian Theology, Harvard Business School and previously held positions at Oriel College, Oxford and at Lancaster University.

The late Barnabas Lindars, SSF, was Rylands Professor, University of Manchester.

Richard Bauckham is Professor of New Testament, University of St Andrews, and a member of the Church of England Doctrine Commission.

Brian Hebblethwaite is Tutor, Queen's College, Cambridge and Lecturer, University of Cambridge.

Adrian Thatcher is Head of the Department of Theology and Religious Studies, College of St Mark and St John, Plymouth.

1. The Resurrection of Jesus: Asking the Right Questions*

Paul Avis

The Resurrection of Jesus Christ is one of the central mysteries of the Christian faith. It is clearly absolutely *central* to Christianity. It shines through almost every book of the New Testament. Take away the Resurrection and you remove the *raison d'être* of the Christian gospel. As Küng puts it: 'Without Easter, there is no faith, no proclamation, no Church, no worship, no mission' (p. 381). But the Resurrection is above all a *mystery*, and a mystery is a challenge to the Christian mind. Faith can never be content with passivity and ignorance – it always seeks understanding of what is presented to it, of what is given (*fides quaerens intellectum*). But in the case of the Resurrection, above all, it behoves us to conduct our enquiry with humility, patience and an open mind. All too often, it seems, discussion of the Resurrection is clouded by blind assertion. There are many who think that they know exactly what the Resurrection was. We are not short of answers – whether they are conservative answers that present the Resurrection as little more than a resuscitation of the corpse of Jesus, or liberal answers, in terms of the survival of Jesus' spirit – that leave us asking how the destiny of Jesus after death differed from that of anyone else. But are they answers to the right questions? Any version of Resurrection faith that presents it merely factually, as an incident in the biography of a human being, is patently inadequate, for it cannot account either for the rise of the Resurrection faith in the disciples, or for its continuance in the believing community (see Selby).

* © Paul Avis 1993

In this volume, various contributors, representing the best of theological scholarship from across the spectrum of theological opinion, explore the doctrine of the Resurrection of Jesus Christ in the New Testament and the theological traditions of the Christian Church. In this introductory chapter I should like to suggest some of the questions that might guide our enquiry and contribute to that process of inexhaustible reflection that the Resurrection provokes. My discussion will be informed by two concerns: to suggest appropriate *boundaries* within which the inevitable speculation on the Resurrection of Jesus Christ might be conducted, and to try to bring into focus the essential *core* and irreducible meaning of the doctrine of the Resurrection.

Can we expect a definitive statement of Christ's Resurrection?

Our first question is whether the nature of the Resurrection can be defined with clarity and precision. From time to time there is clamour among anxious lay members of the Church, aided and abetted by conservative clergy with a thirst for publicity, for the Church's leadership (bishops or synods) to make a clear and definitive pronouncement on what is to be believed about the Resurrection, and thus to put a stop to unsettling controversy in the Church. Is this a realistic demand?

We have to face the fact that it was certainly not a demand that could have been met in New Testament times. C.F. Evans began his book *Resurrection and the New Testament* by reminding us that the Resurrection was controversial in the apostolic age, as 1 Corinthians 15 and 2 Timothy 2:18 clearly indicate. This is not surprising, for the first century BC and the first century AD constituted a period of intense and fervent speculation and controversy in the ancient world about the destiny of the soul after death. The diverse and often incoherent views that were in the air at this time have left their mark on the New Testament writings. St Paul himself is barely consistent on this question, and the Gospels are full of ambiguity. There are discrepancies in the four evangelists as to the location of the Resurrection appearances, their number and order, the number of women and of angels ('young men'). Clearly, there was no concerted effort in the apostolic Church to produce a coherent and consistent account of the Resurrection (Selby, p. 115). The Resurrection continued to be controversial in the post-apostolic age, the second century, and was to provide the Fathers with ample scope for speculation and argument for centuries to come.

It seems to belong to the nature of the Resurrection that it is not susceptible to clear and definitive statement. There are several reasons for this.

First, *the nature of the evidence.* The Gospel narratives and the claims of St Paul in 1 Corinthians 15 are the product of an already complex process of interpretation and tradition. The first Christian writers were incapable of distinguishing between the rise of Resurrection faith in the individual (and the community) and the logic of historical causality. There were, as far as we know, no witnesses present to observe the act of Resurrection itself. Belief in the Resurrection was an inference drawn immediately by the disciples from their experiences of the Risen Christ, and subsequently, and to a lesser extent, from the empty tomb. To reconstruct those experiences the most delicate detective work is required, and even then the results remain fragmentary and conjectural. We cannot even be sure whether it was Mary Magdalene or Simon Peter who was the first to encounter the Risen Christ.

Second, *the nature of the event.* In the New Testament, the Resurrection is neither described nor defended: it is presupposed. It is assumed as the transcendent presupposition of a dynamic and evolving Christology. Christians believe in the Resurrection of Jesus Christ as an act of God. It was God who raised the passive Jesus from the grave. Now, no act of a transcendent God is open to human scrutiny. Even though it impinges on history it eludes the grasp of the historian because it is an act of *God.* If you could capture the mystery of God in a clear and definitive statement, then you could do the same for the Resurrection of Christ.

3

Third, *the nature of faith*. In the New Testament, the Resurrection is proposed for the faith of men and women: 'If you confess with your lips that Jesus is Lord and believe in your heart that God raised him from the dead, you will be saved' (Romans 10:9). Selby has shown that the Resurrection was only credible within the circle of faith and experience of the first Christians, and that belief in the Resurrection is sustained to this day by the corporate life of the Christian community. Of course, our faith is not in a creed, or in an event, but in God. God is the only proper object of faith. But faith in God is not devoid of content. It is faith in God-who-resurrected-Jesus, 'the God and Father of our Lord Jesus Christ' – where the titles Lord (*Kurios*) and Christ (*Xristos*) certainly imply the Resurrection (Ephesians 1:3). Thus, no account of the Resurrection can be adequate that does not require faith. This seems to rule out interpretations that construe the Resurrection in terms of the mere immortality or survival of the human spirit of Jesus after death. But it also follows that, if we could construct a cut-and-dried account of the Resurrection, fitting together the pieces of evidence to make a watertight case, not only would faith be superfluous but the meaning of the Resurrection in the economy of salvation would be undermined. As Carnley has written, over-emphasis on the historical and empirical aspects of Resurrection belief 'may be dogmatically disastrous, for to assimilate the appearance of Jesus to observable events in his life and to his death and burial means that justice can hardly be done to its absolute uniqueness and to its transcendent revelatory nature' (p. 73).

We are bound to conclude, therefore, that it would be neither realistic nor right to hope for a clear and definitive statement of Resurrection belief. While some may find this an unpalatable and uncomfortable conclusion, others may well be excited at the opportunities it opens up for a deeper exploration of an unfathomable mystery. However, to guard against irresponsible speculation, we may need to consider the possibility that there might be appropriate *parameters or boundaries* for Resurrection belief (I have already suggested that the mere survival of the human spirit of Jesus does not do justice to what belief in the Resurrection requires) and that it may be useful to enquire whether there is an *essential core* of Resurrection faith.

What do we mean by 'the Resurrection'?

All Christians believe in 'the Resurrection' of Jesus Christ. The 'liberal' Bishop of Durham, David Jenkins, believes passionately in 'the Resurrection' (though his conservative critics think they believe better and stronger than he does). But simply insisting on 'the Resurrection' gets us nowhere. There is a good deal of unwarranted mystification in some discussions of the subject: for example, at no point in his extensive and eloquent exposition does Moltmann pause to ask what *constitutes* the Resurrection, and Torrance speaks grandiloquently of the Resurrection 'transforming space and time', though we look in vain for any indication of what the empirical correlative of this might be. The focus of faith for all Christians, conservative or liberal or in between, is the same: the God who raised Jesus from death and the Risen Christ who is one with God. But it remains a subject for genuine and necessary enquiry: what do we mean by 'the Resurrection'?

'The Resurrection' is not a description, it is a term established by convention (Hick, p. 171) and includes a range of possible meanings. Basically, 'resurrection' (*anastasis*) is a metaphor deriving from rising to one's feet, standing up, and so wakening from sleep, and 'risen' is a metaphor from *egeirein*, to wake up (Matthew 1:24) or to recover from illness (Mark 1:31). Now, the fact that 'Resurrection' and 'Risen' are metaphors does not imply that they do not refer to something real. Metaphor is used in a highly realist sense to evoke what transcends our everyday more 'factual' language (which is itself made up largely of dead metaphors, that now pass as literal expressions). But metaphorical language entails great fluidity of meaning and breadth of reference. It may be used by different people in different senses.

So when we speak of 'the Resurrection' it is salutary to be aware that we are using an expression, a metaphor, that has

5

been the vehicle for a wealth of varied meaning through the centuries. We cannot assume that we are using it in the same sense as St Paul, and nor can we assume that St Paul was using it in conformity with any particular established usage in Palestinian or Hellenistic Judaism. But it is certainly true that, if we want to know what the New Testament writers meant by the Resurrection, we need to obtain a picture of the emergence of belief in life after death in the Old Testament literature and of the very significant developments that this hope underwent in the intertestamental period. It may well give further food for thought when we discover there precedents for both the highly materialist and physical understanding of the Resurrection in Luke and John and also for the highly spiritual understanding of Paul and certain strands of the Gospel traditions. For this literature speaks of both a resurrection of the body and a resurrection of the spirit without the body (Martin-Achard; Nickelsburg).

The New Testament accounts, read in the light of the intertestamental literature which lie behind them, can sustain several interpretations of what is meant by 'the Resurrection'. They can support, up to a point, a crudely materialist resuscitation theory where Jesus eats in the presence of the disciples – fish and even honeycomb, according to Luke 24:41–43 (so providing evidence even more tangible than that of the Turin Shroud – teeth marks!). Or, at the other end of the spectrum, they can sustain a highly spiritual interpretation where what happened to the body is regarded as irrelevant to the truth of the Resurrection (Paul shows no interest in the empty tomb or the fate of the body).

Evans has reminded us of the elusiveness of the Resurrection, concluding his study by saying that:

> Whatever the Easter event was, it must be supposed to be of such a kind as to be responsible for the production of these traditions as its deposit at whatever remove. The events themselves, however, both the resurrection appearances and the empty tomb, lie so deeply concealed within the traditions that they can be glimpsed only very indirectly, so that the principal difficulty here

6

is not to believe, but to know what it is which offers itself for belief.

To this Selby adds the rider that the Easter event must also have been such as to rule out a *single* interpretation (p. 153).

The term 'Resurrection', then, functions as a *symbol*, close to the centre of Christian belief. It incorporates a variety of intended meanings and is the product of several stages of interpretation. We cannot get behind it to some original pre-linguistic, pre-metaphorical, pre-symbolic account of 'what actually happened' (Schillebeeckx, pp. 392f). To say this is not meant to place a moratorium on further critical enquiry and reconstruction – that is a task that is laid upon the Church's scholars and it does bring results, if not conclusive ones. But it is simply to say that it is salutary to remind ourselves that when we appeal to 'the Resurrection' we are evoking a symbol that, in its plasticity, both unites and divides Christians.

Can belief in the Resurrection be detached from first-century cosmology?

Our third question concerns the authority of the first-century worldview which provided the framework within which the Resurrection faith was articulated. The first Christians' belief in the Resurrection of Jesus was inevitably expressed in terms of the worldview of their day. As we have already noted, that worldview gave them certain concepts of resurrection and immortality, but it also entailed a whole package of assumptions about the world, history and human nature. These assumptions, studied systematically, give us the biblical cosmology, eschatology and anthropology. Today nature, history and human life are studied by the physical, social and life sciences respectively according to very precise methods and criteria. These sciences present us with a very different account to that of the Bible. Is the Resurrection inextricably bound up with the biblical worldview? Can it be detached from first-century cosmology? If it was once interpreted in those terms, is it appropriate to attempt to reinterpret it in ours? After all, the process of interpretation and translation into another culture and set of concepts began immediately, before any of the New Testament books were written, when the original preaching of Jesus in Aramaic and in Hebrew thought-forms (significantly, Hebrew lacked words for nature and body) was transposed into the Greek traditions that make up the New Testament literature.

The ancient world, though by no means totally devoid of scientific interest, was imbued with credulity, superstition and a cavalier disregard for scientific methods of collecting and evaluating evidence. For the early Fathers, the mysteries and miracles of Scripture were paralleled and validated by the mysteries and miracles of nature. Irenaeus pointed out that no one could explain the rise of the Nile, where birds go in winter, the tides, what lies beyond the ocean, the causes of rain, lightning, thunder, clouds, fog, winds, snow, the phases of the moon, why the sea is salty, and so on. Origen believed, like his contemporaries, in the spontaneous generation of snakes from the corpses of men, bees from oxen, wasps from horses, beetles from asses, worms from many things, and in the parthenogenesis of vultures. Tertullian insists that it is sinful pride to attempt to investigate such questions as the shape of the earth. Clement of Rome and Cyril of Jerusalem support the Resurrection of Jesus from the case of the phoenix. Augustine is also genuinely credulous – he is not sure whether Apuleius' changing into an ass and back again is fact or fiction. For him, nature is miraculous throughout (Grant).

In approaching the miracle stories of the New Testament we need to remind ourselves that there was nothing so fantastic that early Christian intellectuals could not believe it. Not even the most conservative contemporary defenders of the physical Resurrection of Jesus would wish to emulate the credulity of the first Christians. Can we find an interpretation of the Resurrection that does not require us to suspend the assumptions on which we operate in every other aspect of life?

Some New Testament accounts assume that the Resurrection – most notably in Luke's physicalist, 'rapture' version

(Schillebeeckx, pp. 340f) – was a translation of the body of Jesus from earth to heaven within a 'three-decker universe'. Indeed, some New Testament cosmologies, those of Ephesians and Colossians, influenced by incipient gnosticism, envisage a hierarchy of spiritual beings ('principalities and powers') above whom Christ ascended to the throne of God. Cosmological speculation of this kind was rife in the apostolic and post-apostolic Church (see Bultmann, 2, pp. 144ff). A layered universe, in which images of transcendence were understood literally, and in which spirit was a refined sort of matter, having a place allocated to it in the cosmos, was the presupposition of Christian doctrine until the Reformation. The Copernican revolution failed to disabuse Luther of his concept of the ubiquity of Christ's body, so fundamental to his sacramental theology, or Calvin of his rival notion that the body was localised in heaven. At the end of the sixteenth century Richard Hooker stated, as though it were self-evident: 'Ascension into heaven is a plain local translation of Christ according to his manhood from the lower to the higher parts of the world' (*Ecclesiastical Polity*, V, lv, 8: Keble edn, 2, p. 244).

Modern cosmology provides a very different world-picture. Western Christians do not believe in a hierarchical cosmos or a local heaven. Christians today well know that, however far into space we explore, we will never come to the end of matter and the beginning of spirit. They believe that the spiritual world belongs to another realm or dimension of reality. What are they to make of the Resurrection? They may well believe that God could raise the body of Jesus from the grave – but what did he do with it on returning to the Father? That is a crucial (and by no means frivolous) question that is not addressed by conservative interpreters of the Resurrection.

Does belief in the Resurrection involve acceptance of New Testament eschatology?

Our fourth question concerns the validity of the form of eschatology (the doctrine of the last things) presupposed by

9

the New Testament Resurrection faith. If the question of cosmology affects mainly the Resurrection and Ascension of Jesus, the question of eschatology is much more far-reaching. Since the work of Weiss and Schweitzer at the end of the last century and the beginning of this, our eyes have been opened to the strongly eschatological context and content of the New Testament. It is apparent that not only St Paul, not only the four evangelists, but Jesus himself thought in eschatological terms derived from late Jewish apocalyptic; that is to say, in terms of radically disjunctive divine action from beyond this world. They expected a decisive act of divine intervention in history that would vindicate the oppressed people of God and destroy their oppressors. This redemptive act would come at the climax of a period of unparalleled tribulation for God's people, but their suffering would not be in vain. Not only would those who remained steadfast under affliction be caught up to share in the joy of the new age, but all the faithful who had died would rise again. The central figure of this scenario and God's agent in judgement/vindication would be the Son of Man, a representative persona in whom the saints were incorporated by divine election.

The claim of T.F. Glasson and J.A.T. Robinson that these are secondary accretions to an original non-apocalyptic message of Jesus has not carried conviction, and C.H. Dodd's theory of 'realised eschatology', while it has valuably drawn attention to those sayings of Jesus that imply that the last things are impinging now and demand decision, has not convinced interpreters that all futurist references are intended to be understood symbolically. Several points have emerged from recent study of New Testament eschatology with reasonable assurance.

Firstly, both Jesus himself and his New Testament interpreters worked within the eschatological assumptions of contemporary Judaism. They thus expected a catastrophic divine intervention in the course of history within a generation or so (Kümmel). But this intervention evidently did not take place in the form that Jesus and the New Testament writers expected.

Secondly, Jesus himself had already transcended the limitations of Jewish apocalyptic: his teaching, though thoroughly eschatological, is free from speculation, sign-watching and fanciful details (Bultmann, 1, p. 5). He did not impart apocalyptic information (Jeremias) or 'predict apocalyptic drama' (Kümmel, p. 152). Furthermore, he made a radical advance on received eschatological assumptions when he announced that the last things were coming to fulfilment now, salvation was at hand now, not only in the future, and that response and decisions *vis-à-vis* himself and his message would be determinative for one's destiny in the great consummation. He was the definitive 'sign of the times' (Bultmann, 1, p. 9); the kingdom of God was embodied in his person (Kümmel, p. 155).

Thirdly, the Resurrection of Jesus would naturally have been interpreted within the available framework. As Jeremias says, 'Judaism did not know of any anticipated resurrection as an event in history. There is nothing comparable to the resurrection of Jesus anywhere in Jewish literature,' except for the resuscitation of individuals (1, p. 308). It is clear, then, that the disciples would have interpreted the Resurrection of Jesus as the dawn of the new age, as the fulfilment of Jewish eschatological hopes. There are clear indications of this in Mark, Matthew and John (Allison). As Jeremias says, the disciples experienced the Resurrection as 'the dawn of the eschaton. . . . They saw Jesus in shining light. They were witnesses of his entry into glory. In other words, *they experienced the parousia*. . . . For the earliest community to believe meant to live here and now in the consummation of the world' (1, p. 310).

Fourthly, when it became apparent that history was continuing, that all things had not come to an end, profound adjustments in the thinking of first-century Christians were called for. The New Testament gives ample evidence of those adjustments taking place. The eschatological framework was not abandoned: though Jesus had not fully consummated the last things, he had definitely inaugurated them. The Resurrection and glorification of Jesus Christ was not, after all, identical with the Parousia: that had been put off into

11

the imminent (early Paul), near (late Paul), or indefinite (2 Peter) future.

Briefly we must ask what abiding validity the eschatological perspective of the New Testament retains for us today. Kümmel has maintained, against Bultmann, that it cannot simply be abandoned and that the message of the New Testament cannot be 'dehistoricised', since eschatology witnesses to the purpose and activity of God in history and this belongs to the essence of the New Testament (p. 148). In his *Theology of Hope* Moltmann is deceptively radical. He uses the rhetoric of eschatology to undermine eschatology by reinterpreting it in Christological terms, thus:

> For what God has made manifest, according to the statements of the Easter narratives, was not the course of history, not the secrets of the higher world of heaven, not the outcome of the future world judgement, but the future of the crucified Christ for the world. (pp. 192f)

Moltmann insists that 'Christian eschatology is not Christianised apocalyptic' and that 'Christian eschatology which seeks to span the inexhaustible future of Christ, does not set the event of the Resurrection within a framework of apocalyptic and world history.' Rather, it asks what God is saying ('intends') in raising him (pp. 193f). I agree with Moltmann's conclusions, that the Resurrection points to Christology, not to a revelation of God's 'plans' for world history, but I disapprove of the way Moltmann dresses up his argument in eschatological rhetoric. Moltmann has frankly abandoned eschatology. A contentless 'hope', one that does not specify its empirical 'cash value', is no substitute.

Is it not better all round to accept that modern theology works without an eschatology in the first-century sense? Modern Christian faith does not require one. It is much more concerned with the question of theodicy than the question of a literal eschatology. It asks whether and how God is present in suffering, not what he has up his sleeve that will supervene on the historical process. But this sets the Resurrection in a different light. In an eschatological perspective, the Resurrection appears as the final act of world history and the coming to birth of a new age. The faithful remnant, still living on the earth, will share in it – and that implies a physical rapture (1 Thessalonians 4: 13–17). But in the perspective of theodicy, the Resurrection witnesses to the involvement of God in human suffering and contains the promise that he will gather the oppressed to himself in spite of their having perished without seeing God's salvation. This is a spiritual transaction and the relevance of the empty tomb is not readily apparent. The intertestamental work The Wisdom of Solomon anticipates this modern approach:

> The souls of the just are in God's hand and torment shall not touch them. In the eyes of foolish men they seemed to be dead; their departure was reckoned as defeat and their going from us as disaster. But they are at peace, for though in the sight of men they may be punished, they have a sure hope of immortality; and after a little chastisement they will receive great blessings, because God has tested them and found them worthy to be his. (3:1–5)

This is of course still, strictly speaking, eschatology, but it is an eschatology that looks for its fulfilment beyond this world and after this life, rather than within the structures of this world and the present form of human existence.

What is essential in Resurrection faith?

Our fifth question concerns the appropriate limits of speculation and the irreducible essence of Resurrection faith. If, as I have suggested, we cannot realistically expect a clear and definitive statement of what happened at the Resurrection of Jesus, it becomes all the more pertinent to ask whether there are any parameters or boundaries within which genuine Resurrection faith can be located, and whether there is an essential core of Resurrection belief that is vital to the Christian faith. What is crucial for faith in the Resurrection?

On one side of the argument I would propose the parameter that the Resurrection is *no mere resuscitation of the corpse of Jesus.* Jewish thought could cope with resuscitation, as we see in the Elijah and Elisha sagas and the raising of

13

Jairus' daughter, the widow of Nain's son and Lazarus in the Gospels. These were resurrections to *mortal* life. It is true that elements of intertestamental, Pharisaic and patristic thought took resurrection so literally that it became little more than the body returning to life and carrying on. But in Jewish thought the resuscitations were not eschatological, they were not what the new age of God's redemption would bring. There are, of course, crudely literalistic elements in the Gospels, especially Luke and John, that could be construed in terms of resuscitation, but these are counteracted by the more ethereal elements in the Gospel narratives and by St Paul, for whom the body of the Resurrection, the 'spiritual body', can only be described by the vaguest of analogies (1 Corinthians 15:35–44). Though the risen Lord was possessed of a body, it was a 'glorious body' (Philippians 3:20f), a transformed body (see Gundry, ch. 13; Moule). Pannenberg insists that it is 'absolutely certain' that the resurrection of the dead was not understood as mere resuscitation 'in the primitive Christian and, in any case, in the oldest, the Pauline, concept' (p. 75). It is extremely difficult to see what resurrection as resuscitation could mean theologically or what significance it could have for faith. It would be a mere freak, a paranormal phenomenon, devoid of transcendent import.

On the other side of the argument I would propose the parameter that the Resurrection is *no mere survival of the spirit of Jesus*. It is not a case of simple immortality. However, it is certainly not less than this: it is intrinsic to orthodox Christian faith to hold that God has created humanity in the divine image, that is to say, as spirit; that this spirit (at least in those who are quickened by divine grace) is imperishable; and that it returns to God after the death of the body. I think I could make little sense of a version of the Christian faith that taught that this earthly life is all there is, thereby removing the mainspring of our earthly pilgrimage which is the hope of the vision of God and the consummation of our union with God. But we do not need the Resurrection to bring us the hope of life beyond death. As Hick has pointed out:

> The idea that Jesus' resurrection provides the Christian's sole ground for belief in a life after death cannot be sustained historically. . . . Jesus' disciples believed in life after death before and independently of his resurrection; and much Christian theology has since affirmed the immortality of the soul on grounds which do not rely on the Easter message. Jesus' resurrection does of course support and confirm belief in the continuity of man's life beyond physical death; but it is probably only in the modern period, when the assurance of survival has waned, that it has occurred to anyone to point to Jesus' resurrection as a primary ground for belief in a life to come. (p. 178)

To reduce the Resurrection to the survival of the immortal spirit of Jesus which then returns to God makes his destiny no different from that of any other person – or perhaps I should say, any believer (we do not want to embark on the universalist question here!). Moltmann rightly insists that it is not a 'symbol of the hope for immortality' (p. 208). Furthermore, it requires little faith to believe it. The nature of the Resurrection must answer to the nature of the human condition marked by alienation, frustration and guilt. It must also answer to the profundity of the cross of Christ as a great drama, transaction and enactment between God, Christ and humanity. As Hoskyns perceptively wrote:

> To St Paul this whole situation is not met by a brave belief in immortality, and certainly not by a belief in the immortality of the soul. To discard the word 'resurrection' means to St Paul to move away from the horror of sin at the very point at which it is most essential that it should be taken seriously. (p. 125)

Not a crude resuscitation of the flesh, but a new creation in which sin is destroyed and new life is unleashed is demanded by the logic of Crucifixion–Resurrection.

If then the Resurrection is more than mere resuscitation or survival, what is this 'more'? It will point us in the right direction if we bear in mind that the Resurrection must answer to the cross of Christ – to who it was who died and why he died – to the *cross* of *Christ*.

First, *who was it that died?* It was no mere individual but a corporate, representative figure – the Son of Man, the Messiah, the one whose destiny was interlocked with that of his people who by faith, baptism and the Holy Spirit are 'in' him in the sight of God, united with him so fully and finally that it can be said that he died for their sakes and they died and rose in him (Galatians 2:20; Romans 6:3–8). Furthermore, as mediator between God and humanity he represents and embodies not only his people but God himself in his saving purpose. He is the one, therefore, in whom God himself entered into mortality, suffering and death. Jesus' cause was the cause of God. In his ministry and mission God was present and at work. His proclamation, 'The kingdom of God is at hand,' was a Hebraic reverential circumlocution for 'God himself has drawn near to you' (Jeremias, 1, p. 102).

Second, *why did he die?* He died not merely a martyr's death, bearing witness to the truth. Nor was he wiped out pointlessly, like so many others who happened to be in the wrong place at the wrong time. Nor was he merely the defenceless victim of injustice. Jesus embraced his destiny. In his self-emptying and self-surrender he plumbed the depths of our human alienation, frustration and guilt. His own understanding of his destiny was shaped by reflection on the suffering servant figure of the book of Isaiah. This means that, even if he did not actually predict the Resurrection 'on the third day', he trusted in God to vindicate him and to take up his suffering and death into God's redemptive purposes and to give him glory (Isaiah 53:10–12).

In the light of the questions, who was it that died on the cross, and why?, we must make the affirmation of Christian theology that Crucifixion–Resurrection was a drama internal to the life of God. As Moltmann writes:

> The death of Jesus was experienced as the death of him who had been sent as the Messiah of God, and therefore implies also the 'death of God'. Thus his death is experienced and proclaimed as god-forsakenness, as judgement, as curse, as exclusion from the promised life, as reprobation and damnation.

Correspondingly, the Resurrection must be understood as

the 'conquest of the deadliness of death ... of god-forsaken-ness ... of judgement and of the curse, as a beginning of the fulfilment of the promised life, and thus as a conquest of all that is dead in death ... as a negation of the negation of God' (pp. 210f).

The essence of Resurrection faith is contained in the affirmation that in the Resurrection Jesus was made one with God after his death and that this union was total and definitive, requiring the traditional Christian vocabulary of the beatific vision and of perfected union with God (most familiarly represented to us in the consummation of Dante's vision). The spirit of Jesus did not languish in the abode of departed spirits, the shades and figments of the Greek Hades and the Hebrew Sheol. Neither did he continue his journey ever nearer to the presence of God, as we might imagine is the pilgrimage destined for Christian souls after death. He was translated 'immediately' and without reservation, as it were, to glory and became one with the Father.

The New Testament seems to be saying something very close to this when it speaks of the glorification, or enthrone-ment, of Christ at the Resurrection (Philippians 2:9f; Acts 2:33; Hebrews 1:36; 1 Peter 3:22), and it has been suggested that this represents the earliest version of Resurrection faith. As Evans observes, 'There are passages in the New Testament which virtually ignore resurrection and pass straight to an exaltation to God or to his right hand' (p. 135). In Paul (and also in Luke) the drama, the transaction between God, Christ and humanity, takes place explicitly in the realm of the Spirit. The *Holy Spirit* is the agent of the Resurrection (Romans 1:4) and imparts the resurrection life to believers (Romans 8:11); the Risen Christ exists in the mode of the Spirit, as it were, and comes to meet his people in the Spirit (1 Corinthians 15:45; 2 Corinthians 3:17).

What is essential in Resurrection faith? It is that *through the Holy Spirit Jesus Christ is both one with the Father in glory and one with his people on earth.* His godmanhood, that has plumb-ed the depths of our alienation, frustration and guilt, has passed victoriously through death and is now one with God. But in this unity with God his identity is preserved: he is still

17

the embodiment of God's sovereignty (*autobasilea*); he is the Lord (*Kyrios*). As one with God, the ascended Christ is the judge of all; as one with us, he is our compassionate and merciful high priest, mediator and advocate. *The Risen Christ is the one who unites us with God.*

Must I believe in the Resurrection to be a Christian?

Our final question concerns the degree of explicit belief in the Resurrection of Christ that is necessary to regard oneself (and be regarded by the Church) as a Christian. This question is motivated by a pastoral concern for those individuals in the churches or on the fringes who find the supernatural paraphernalia of Christianity a stumbling block to faith. Pastoral experience suggests that there are many who can make the central affirmation of Christianity – 'God was in Christ reconciling the world to himself' (2 Corinthians 5:19) – but who find the miraculous accompaniments of this saving presence of God in Jesus not only utterly incredible but also totally meaningless. They have a faith, but it does not include the virginal conception, the physical resurrection, the nature miracles of Jesus, the Ascension and the second coming. Are they entitled to call themselves Christians? Can the Church recognise them as such? Must one believe in the Resurrection to be a Christian? Several points for reflection suggest themselves.

When the fishermen, tax collectors and others heeded the call of Jesus to enter into discipleship with him, there was no hint of resurrection to come. It is, of course, true that there was no shadow of the Cross either at that time. But there was a real discipleship there as they responded to the one who was invested with the authority of God to preach the gospel, heal the sick and reconstitute the people of God. Some modern interpreters (notably Marxen) have attempted to swing the centre of gravity in Christology back from the Resurrection to the ministry of Jesus. This is a useful corrective if it reminds us that it is only who Jesus is, the gospel he preached and embodied, and the ministry he performed that gives meaning to the Resurrection. The

18

Resurrection is not a prodigy, nor is it the work of a *deus ex machina*. It does not reverse the Crucifixion, but completes it and enables it to shine out. The Resurrection does not stand on its own ground but on that of the ministry leading up to the Passion. As Abraham says to the rich man in torment in the parable of Dives and Lazarus, 'If they do not hear Moses and the prophets, neither will they be convinced if someone should rise from the dead' (Luke 16:31). Nicholas Lash could be commenting on this text when he writes:

> If the manner of his living, and teaching, and dying, affords no basis for that trust in him which is, simultaneously, trust in the One who sends him and speaks to us through him, then nothing that happens to the disciples (or to us) after Jesus' death can be such as to warrant confessing him as the Christ of God. (p. 180)

I believe that there could be a faith without explicit belief in the Resurrection as a divine act. It would be the sort of faith that the disciples might have retained after the disaster of Good Friday. They could never have forgotten how Jesus had brought them closer to God. Their hearts had burned within them as he walked with them in the way even then. There would have remained a deeper faith in the God of Israel to whom the Old Testament books bore witness. They would have attempted an imitation of Christ and retained a sense that God was always near to cherish the oppressed. A trust in God that transcended suffering, darkness and death might have been left to them. But it would have been a sombre, indeed a tragic, faith – the quality of faith that could say with Job, 'Though he slay me yet will I trust in him.' There would have been faith and charity but little hope.

Peter Vardy has recently suggested that Resurrection belief is the criterion of an authentic Christian theology. Up to a point I agree. There is no question but that the Easter faith is the living heart of Christian faith. As Küng bluntly puts it, 'Without Easter there is no gospel' (p. 381). However, I could certainly envisage a version of the Christian faith (and, to be frank, Christian theism has shown itself to be almost infinitely flexible) in which the outcome of the death of

19

Jesus was not seen as any different from that of other human beings. This solidarity could be regarded as an aspect of the Incarnation. The outcome would be interpreted in terms of a moral victory over evil, a sacrifice of one's life in the cause of God which is also the cause of humanity, the soul gathered to God. In my opinion a person holding such views about the Resurrection would still be a Christian believer, provided that he or she could affirm with the New Testament that 'God was in Christ reconciling the world to himself.' The life and death of Jesus would have to be seen as a special, perhaps unique, instrument of the gracious purposes of God.

In this interpretation, the fact of the Incarnation, rather than any particular interpretation of the Resurrection, would be the touchstone of Christian faith and Christian theology, and what is believed about the Resurrection would be brought into line with what many already believe about the virginal conception. Thus I agree with Küng when he says, 'If someone still has no idea or very little idea of what to make of the miracle of the resurrection, of the new life, but regards this Jesus as the ultimate criterion of his mortal life and finite death and thus as living, then it cannot be denied that he is a Christian' (p. 380). The Resurrection is not the criterion of discipleship or of Christian profession, though it is intrinsic to a fully fledged Christian faith and theology.

As we have seen, the Resurrection faith speaks of much more than the survival of the soul of Jesus, his spirit gathered to God like that of others. It speaks of a drama, a transaction, an enactment in the realm of the Holy Spirit which releases new life for those who are 'in Christ' so that he may be also 'in' them. It speaks of the definitive unity between Jesus and God and Jesus and ourselves. In that understanding, the fate of the physical body of Jesus (and it is that approach to the Resurrection which constitutes the stumbling block for many) plays little part, for the empty tomb provides neither proof nor meaningful content for the Resurrection. In itself it is ambiguous and inconclusive. It may be an eloquent symbol, but it is not the reality of Resurrection. In the earliest account, that of Mark 16:1–8, the empty tomb creates not faith and understanding but fear and terror (Küng, p. 365). It still takes faith to believe that he who hung on the cross is one with the glory of God and one with us in the depths of our being. But it is the right kind of faith – faith in the Father, Son and Holy Spirit – rather than faith in a phenomenon, an event, a claim. Anyone who has that kind of faith is not far from the kingdom of God.

Bibliography

Allison, D.C., *The End of the Ages Has Come* (Edinburgh: T & T Clark, 1987)

Bultmann, R., *Theology of the New Testament* (2 vols; London: SCM, 1952)

Carnley, P., *The Structure of Resurrection Belief* (Oxford: Clarendon Press, 1987)

Evans, C.F., *Resurrection and the New Testament* (London: SCM, 1970)

Grant, R.M., *Miracle and Natural Law in Graeco-Roman and Early Christian Thought* (Amsterdam, 1952)

Gundry, R.H., *Sōma in Biblical Theology* (Cambridge: Cambridge University Press, 1976)

Hick, J., *Death and Eternal Life* (London: Fount, 1979)

Hoskyns, E.C. and Davey, F.N., *Crucifixion–Resurrection* (ed. G. Wakefield; London: SPCK, 1981)

Jeremias, J., *New Testament Theology* (2 vols; London: SCM, 1971)

Kümmel, W.G., *Promise and Fulfilment: The Eschatological Message of Jesus* (2nd edn; London: SCM, 1961)

Küng, H., *On Being a Christian* (London: Collins, 1977)

Künneth, W., *The Theology of the Resurrection* (London: SCM, 1965)

Lash, N., *Theology on the Way to Emmaus* (London: SCM, 1986)

Martin-Achard, R., *From Death to Life: A Study of the Development of the Doctrine of the Resurrection in the Old Testament* (Edinburgh: Oliver & Boyd, 1960)

Marxen, W., *The Resurrection of Jesus of Nazareth* (Philadelphia: Fortress Press; London: SCM, 1970)

Moltmann, J., *Theology of Hope* (London: SCM, 1967)

Moule, C.F.D., 'St Paul and Dualism: The Pauline Conception of the Resurrection', *New Testament Studies*, 12 (1966), pp. 106–23

Moule, C.F.D. (ed.), *The Significance of the Message of the Resurrection for Faith in Jesus Christ* (London: SCM, 1968)

Nickelsburg, G.W.E., *Resurrection, Immortality and Eternal Life in Intertestamental Judaism* (Cambridge, Mass: Harvard University Press; London: Oxford University Press, 1972)

Pannenberg, W., *Jesus: God and Man* (London: SCM, 1968)

Schillebeeckx, E., *Jesus: An Experiment in Christology* (London: Collins, 1979)

Selby, P., *Look for the Living* (London: SCM, 1976)

Torrance, T.F., *Space, Time and Resurrection* (Edinburgh: Handsel Press, 1976)

Vardy, P., *God of our Fathers? Do we know what we believe?* (London: Darton, Longman & Todd, 1987)

I am grateful to Dr John Muddiman for commenting on an earlier draft of this paper.

2. The Meaning of the Resurrection of Jesus*

Paul Badham

The traditional view

For most of the Christian centuries the Resurrection of Jesus Christ was thought to be a perfectly intelligible belief, whose meaning was self-evident, and whose acceptance was a basic condition of Christian identity. One of the clearest expressions of this historic faith comes in the fourth Anglican Article: 'Christ did truly rise again from death, and took again his body, with flesh, bones, and all things pertaining to the perfection of Man's nature; wherewith he ascended into heaven, and there sitteth.' This understanding of Jesus' Resurrection was seen as having one supremely important implication for his followers, namely that it guaranteed a like destiny for us. What happened to Jesus then would happen to us all at the end of time. The 'particles composing each individual's flesh' would be collected together, the sea would 'give up its dead', the cannibal restore the flesh he had borrowed, and the identical structure which death had previously destroyed would be raised to new life.[1] This understanding of Jesus' Resurrection and its implications for us was affirmed in the Apostles' Creed with its dual assertion of the Resurrection of Jesus and of the resurrection of the flesh (*carnis*). This pattern of belief was declared *de fide* for the Western Church by the Fourth Lateran Council (1215) and for the Orthodox by St John Damascene's *Exact Exposition of the Orthodox Faith*; it was the traditional teaching of the Church of England as shown by the Book of Homilies

* © Paul Badham 1993

and by Hooker; it was taught in Calvin's *Institutes*, and in Luther's small Catechism.[2] There is, therefore, a good prima-facie case for a traditionally minded Christian to say that there is no doubt about the meaning of the Resurrection of Jesus; the problem is simply that many who think of themselves as Christians have ceased to believe in it.

Why alternatives are necessary

There are two grounds for saying that the traditional view should not be regarded as the only possible Christian perspective on this matter: firstly, as demonstrated by other contributors to this volume, it is far from clear that the traditional interpretation of the meaning of the Resurrection of Jesus is the only perspective to be found in the New Testament; secondly, it is clear that many contemporary Christians do profoundly believe in what they refer to as 'the Resurrection' without wishing to endorse every aspect of the traditional picture. The question to be resolved is whether or not alternatives to the traditional understanding can be regarded as having sufficient in common with it to count as authentic doctrines of 'Resurrection' rather than as beliefs which ought more appropriately to be described in other ways.

This is a real problem with a belief as central to Christianity as the Resurrection of Jesus Christ, for all who profess and call themselves Christians have to acknowledge that belief in the Resurrection was historically decisive in the origins of Christianity, and that it is at the centre of almost all forms of Christian worship. To deny the Resurrection would therefore be to cut oneself off from the Christian community. Hence, if one values one's membership of the Christian community, one will consciously or unconsciously interpret what one does believe as being 'the meaning' or at least 'a meaning' of the Resurrection. It is up to the Churches' own official spokespersons to say whether or not any putative claim concerning the meaning of the Resurrection is, or is not, acceptable within their understanding of the framework of faith. I cannot fulfil that role. What I do propose to do is to look at some of the 'meanings' which have been given to the Resurrection of Jesus and consider whether or not they are sufficiently near to the historic claim to count as reinterpretations, rather than denials, of what lies at the heart of historic Christianity.

Explaining the traditional position
Let us start from the most straightforward use of Resurrection language. Etymologically, the English word 'resurrection' is a transliteration of the Latin for 'rising again' and is used in New Testament translations for the Greek word *anastasis* which literally means 'standing up'. The credal clause, 'We look for the resurrection of the dead' could be more literally translated, 'We look for the standing up again of the corpses.' This primal meaning is present in many of the New Testament texts relating to the Resurrection of Jesus. The point of the empty tomb narratives is that the body of Jesus was no longer there because he had been 'raised up'. We note the juxtaposition of talk of Jesus having risen from the dead with talk of the place where he had lain. We hear of his tomb being empty and the grave clothes scattered.[3] We hear of Mary Magdalene being asked to stop clinging to Jesus, and of Thomas being invited to touch him.[4] There seems little doubt that such passages imply a concept of resurrection of a very physical and straightforward kind. This is explicitly spelt out in Luke 24:38–43 where, faced with the disciples' apparent belief that they were seeing a spirit (*pneuma*), the risen Christ is described as saying, 'Why do questionings rise in your hearts? See my hands and my feet, that it is I myself; handle me and see; for a spirit has not flesh and bones as you see that I have.' Then, finding the disciples still incredulous, Jesus asked for something to eat, and was given a piece of broiled fish which he ate in their presence to prove the actuality of his physical presence. The meaning here is consciously and unambiguously an assertion of a literal rising up from the dead, and this is a primary source of the unbroken tradition of a physical understanding of the Resurrection of Jesus as the dominant Christian interpretation of what happened on the first Easter morning.

Linking Jesus' Resurrection to ours

To interpret the Resurrection of Jesus in so directly a physical manner raises the question of what happened subsequently to his risen body. It is therefore no accident that Luke, who so stresses the physicality of Christ's Resurrection, also goes on to assert a physical lifting up (ascension) of Jesus' body into a localised heaven in the sky.[5] In the historic Christian tradition the two beliefs are intimately woven together and used as primary grounds for expecting the literal physical resurrection and ascension of all the human race at the end of time. This is explicitly stated by Polycarp, Ignatius, Justin, Irenaeus, Tertullian, the Apostolic Constitutions, Cyprian, Eusebius, Pamphilius, Augustine, Rufinus and Jerome,[6] and, as we have already noted, such a view was taken into the universal Christian tradition of both East and West, Protestant and Catholic.

One problem with this view is that the schema as a whole is no longer credible. Belief in a literal heaven to which a resurrected earthly body could be carried by clouds is so much at variance with what we know about the nature of reality as to be almost unthinkable for contemporary Christians. So much so, in fact, that many instinctively wish to disassociate Christianity from such naivety, and even, with Alan Richardson,[7] deny that biblical writers held such views. Such escapism will not do. Detailed study of intertestamental Judaism, first-century Christianity, and early Patristic writings makes it crystal clear that belief in upward ascension to a relatively near heaven posed no conceptual difficulties to the early believers.[8] Similarly with the belief in the literal reassembling of every particle of every corpse; this seemed to the early Fathers to be a completely intelligible and reasonable hope. But once again it is a hope so much at variance with what we know today about the nature of human life that very few Christians find it possible to take it seriously. That Cranmer arbitrarily altered the English of the Apostles' Creed in the most often-used services, from affirming the resurrection of the flesh to affirming instead the resurrection of the body, has been very fortunate for English-speaking Christians as it has made reinterpretation at a subconscious level possible, and many are thus unaware of their divergence from earlier forms of Christianity. But however that may be, the point is clear that the traditional understanding of Jesus' Resurrection as the literal uprising of his old body is associated with a framework of understanding few Christians today find acceptable. Hence the most straightforward understanding of the Resurrection has been generally abandoned.

The mainstream position today

The most popular modification of traditional Christianity suggests that Jesus' Resurrection be understood as meaning that he rose from the dead in a new spiritual body which was in some sense continuous with the body laid in the tomb. This is expressed most clearly by C.F.D. Moule, who suggests that 'The material of which the body [i.e. the corpse of Jesus] was composed was somehow transformed into a different mode of existence.'[9] One ground for thinking this is that while all the Gospel accounts report that Jesus' tomb was empty, they also suggest that there was something very unusual about Jesus' risen body. He was able to pass through locked doors, and to appear and disappear at will;[10] the disciples seem to have had difficulty in recognising him, and when they did they felt a sense of awe in his presence. Thus Thomas cried out in adoration, 'My Lord and my God,' and at the disciples' last meeting with Jesus, as recorded in Matthew, we are told that some worshipped Jesus.[11] Moreover, the whole impact of the Resurrection in the New Testament was quite other than the reported responses to other believed raisings of the dead. Jesus was not raised from the dead like Jairus's daughter, or the Widow of Nain's son, or Lazarus.[12] Rather, Jesus' Resurrection was acclaimed by St Paul as a cosmic event in which 'Death is swallowed up; victory is won!'[13]

To interpret Jesus' Resurrection as meaning that he was not simply resuscitated, but rather was raised up to new and glorious life in a spiritual body, seems to give fuller meaning to the Resurrection hope than the traditional account. It

27

does justice both to the empty tomb tradition, and to the unusual elements in the accounts of Jesus' appearances. It also provides for a Resurrection hope for Christians who may suppose, with St Paul in Philippians 3:21, that: 'He will transfigure the body belonging to our humble state, and give it a form like that of his own resplendent body, by the power which enables him to make all things subject to himself.' Taken as a whole it is not surprising that this understanding of the Resurrection of Jesus should be endorsed by the House of Bishops of the Church of England as expressing its faith.[14]

Some problems with a 'spiritual body'

Not all Christians are happy with this concept of a 'spiritual body'. Don Cupitt has argued that this understanding of a 'spiritual body' is a logical hybrid, a combination of mutually incompatible terms like 'a square circle'.[15] For the Resurrection body is considered to be sufficiently bodily to be seen, heard, and wear clothes, and yet at the same time thought to be sufficiently spiritual to pass through locked doors. How can it simultaneously possess these mutually incompatible characteristics? Consider also the question of the broiled fish; are we to suppose that a spiritual body needs such sustenance? If it does, how can it then immediately disappear through the walls? Was the newly ingested fish instantly spiritualised so that it too could pass through the walls? It may seem crude to press such issues, but they need to be faced if one is to take the notion of a spiritual body seriously. And even if we feel able to accept that a spiritual body could itself behave in the ways required by the stories, the question of its clothes raises further problems. No one imagines that the Risen Christ appeared naked to his disciples in the upper room, or to Cleopas and his companion on the road to Emmaus, or to Mary Magdalene in the garden. Yet to suppose that earthly clothes are integral to the being of a spiritual body, so that clothes and body together can appear and disappear through locked doors, is a very bizarre notion.

Another problem is that this interpretation of the spiritual body hypothesis may not harmonise with the empty tomb traditions as easily as its defenders suppose. For if a spiritual body is designed to be the means of our embodiment in a new and glorious life in heaven, and if freedom from the limitations of earthly existence is integral to it, then the matter of which Jesus' corpse was composed should be irrelevant to it. The House of Bishops of the Church of England point out that, 'Our Lord's own crucified body must have undergone irreversible physiological changes very shortly after death,' and therefore the Bishops suggest that re-creation is a better model for the future hope than resuscitation. They add that awareness of the radical difference between the two modes of being 'helps to relate our own resurrection, where the question of an empty tomb does not arise, more intelligibly to that of Jesus'.[16] But there is an unresolved tension in this argument. The Bishops rightly affirm that an integral part of the New Testament message is that Jesus' Resurrection is the foundation for our future hope. But in this context an asymmetry between our corpses which are destroyed and decomposed, and Jesus' body which was transformed and raised up, becomes serious. In fact, a spiritual body might be a better foundation for our future hope if it were not always linked in people's minds to faith in the empty tomb and belief in such physical elements in the appearance stories as the accounts of Jesus eating fish. Much Easter Day preaching is vitiated by the fact that arguments in favour of the empty tomb of Jesus are used as grounds for our confidence in a future life, even though our tombs are supposedly to remain full.

A spiritual Resurrection

A third understanding of the Resurrection tackles these problems by focusing entirely on the appearances of Jesus and discounting the empty tomb and the eating fish traditions. On this view the spiritual body is unequivocally spiritual, and is a way of saying that Jesus' essential personality, or soul, survived death and communicated the fact of his victory over death to the minds of the disciples through a series of visionary experiences. It is these visionary experiences which came to be written up as the Resurrection appearances. Over the years the disciples' insistence on the reality of what they had encountered led to their reports being increasingly interpreted in more and more 'physical' ways. But this was not true of the earliest tradition.

To many contemporary Christians the view I have just described will seem like a denial rather than an affirmation of Easter, and indeed, in so far as it rejects the testimony of the empty tomb, it will be repudiating a belief which has for nineteen hundred years been taken for granted as a basic symbol of Resurrection faith. Nevertheless, the view I have described could be regarded as expressing a Resurrection hope if it could be shown as articulating a New Testament perspective, and as sustaining living faith in the Christian hope today.

St Paul's view

The case for focusing on the appearances of Jesus and for interpreting them as visionary experiences centres on the belief that this was St Paul's understanding. Since Paul is very much our earliest witness his views can be taken as representing the understanding of Easter of the very earliest Christians which gave rise to the birth of the Christian movement. It seems clear that Paul explicitly uses Resurrection language in a non-literal sense, for he affirms resurrection while denying that 'flesh and blood' can ever experience it and while declaring that our stomachs will permanently perish.[17] Moreover, it is significant that Paul appends his own experience on the road to Damascus to something that looks like an official list of the Resurrection appearances of Jesus.[18] This suggests that St Paul regarded what happened to him as being of the same type as the experiences of the first apostles. Yet St Paul's experience was explicitly not a question of straightforward seeing, for although the three reports in Acts are confused and contradictory, they all agree that Paul's companions did not fully share in his experience.[19] Paul himself described it as a revelation: 'God revealed his son to me' is what he says, and the Greek is *en emoi* which literally means 'within me'.[20] Elsewhere St Paul describes his experience as 'a heavenly vision' or 'an appearance'.[21] This latter term is of considerable significance, for most New Testament scholars believe that the word *ophthe*, which is translated here as 'appearance', refers to spiritual vision rather than to ocular sighting.[22] Hence it is very interesting that St Paul should use the word *ophthe* in his 'official list' of Christ's appearances as well as to describe what he himself experienced.

A good case can be made for saying that for St Paul the meaning of Christ's Resurrection should be understood in a non-physical way. He believed that to ask the question of how dead bodies can be raised was 'a senseless question'.[23] For him, resurrection necessarily implied rising to a wholly new kind of life. Consider the sustained contrast he makes between the two modes of existence: earthly is contrasted with heavenly, perishable with imperishable, humiliation with glory, weakness with power, and animal with spiritual.[24] Such contrasts would be wholly beside the point if St Paul had understood resurrection in terms of physical rising.

In Philippians 1:22–24 Paul declares himself 'torn two ways' between his desire 'to depart' (from this life) in order to 'be with Christ', and his wish to 'stay on in the body' for the sake of his fellow Christians. St Paul expresses the same view in 2 Corinthians 5:8, where he says he would like to leave his home in the body to go to live with the Lord. Such a sentiment does not make any kind of sense except on the supposition that Paul took for granted that Jesus had also permanently left his home in the body. Paul had no doubt that this Jesus, who had left his home in the body, was really alive and had really triumphed over death. His encounter with this Christ transformed his whole life and, as he told King Agrippa, he could never be 'disobedient to that heavenly vision'.[25] Yet Paul was quite sure it was no resuscitated corpse he had seen, but rather a vision of the glory that lies ahead, for whereas it was a physical body that was buried, it was a spiritual body that was raised.[26] St Paul was not alone in this understanding of the meaning of resurrection, for a similar position seems to be expounded by the author of

31

the first letter of Peter who writes, 'In the body [Jesus] was put to death; in the spirit he was brought to life.'[27]

The empty tomb as a late tradition

To suggest that a resolutely 'spiritual' account of the Resurrection represents the original meaning presupposes that the empty tomb narratives were not part of the earliest tradition. The case for such a presupposition is partly the priority of Paul, and partly the indirect testimony of our earliest Gospel. Almost all scholars agree both that St Mark's Gospel is the earliest, and that the best-authenticated texts of his Gospel end at Chapter 16, verse 8. Mark's Gospel ends with an account of the women discovering the empty tomb and then the astounding comment that 'they said nothing to anyone about this, for they were afraid'. A literal translation of the Greek is even stronger: 'No one, no anything, they told.' Such a comment cannot make any kind of sense unless the story of the women finding the tomb empty was no part of the original Easter kerygma. If everyone knew that the women had reported finding an empty tomb, Mark's comment would have been an absurdity. It makes sense only on the supposition that Mark was consciously adding something to the original kerygma, and hence has to give some explanation as to why no one had previously heard this empty tomb story before.

Advantages of a spiritual interpretation

To suggest that the original meaning of Jesus' Resurrection was that his essential personality had triumphed over the destruction of his body has one further advantage. It can help to safeguard the New Testament view that the Resurrection is a foundation for our own future hope. Many Christians today agree with the Church of England Doctrine Commission that,

> We ought to reject quite frankly the literalistic belief in a future
> resuscitation of the actual physical frame which is laid in the
> tomb ... none the less ... in the life of the world to come
> the soul or spirit will still have its organ of expression and activity,

which is one with the body of earthly life in the sense that it
bears the same relation to the same spiritual entity.[28]

This view holds that the self continues through death, even
though it also affirms that, for full personhood to exist, the
soul or spirit must at some point be clothed upon by a new
body. This may have been St Paul's view too, for although
he talks on two occasions of departing from his present
body, his use of such terminology in no sense implies an
expectation that he would live henceforth in a disembodied
state. On the contrary, he insists that in our new condition,
'we shall not find ourselves naked', but rather our 'inner
nature' will have a new body put on over it so that our
mortal part may be absorbed into life immortal'.[29] On this
interpretation, what St Paul deduces as the implication of
Christ's Resurrection corresponds to what contemporary
Christians in the main expect to happen. Hence this 'spiritual' interpretation of the Resurrection might have a better
case for being regarded as 'good news' or 'Gospel' than the
traditional literal view which many find impossible to believe,
or the mainstream view endorsed by the House of Bishops
which tends to divorce what is affirmed concerning Jesus
from what is hoped for as the future state of Christians.
However, each of these three ways of interpreting the Resurrection of Jesus can be said to affirm the basic meaningful-
ness of a victory of Jesus over death. Each can be
characterised as 'objective' accounts of the Resurrection in
that they affirm that something happened to Jesus independently of the faith of the first disciples. Our ultimate commitment to one or other of these hypotheses, or our rejection
of all three, will probably owe as much to our assessment of
what is possible as to our detailed study of the biblical texts.

The case for a subjective approach

The primary case for a subjective approach to the Resurrection is that many thinkers who are personally committed to
the Christian faith find it frankly impossible to continue
to believe in any of the Resurrection claims we have been

discussing. Rudolf Bultmann acknowledged the situation quite openly. He was convinced that 'resurrection from the dead is utterly inconceivable'. It could never be established as remotely possible, 'no matter how many witnesses are cited'. His rejection was not simply of the traditional view of the raising up of Jesus' dead body, but also of more sophisticated notions such as the 'clothing of the human personality . . . with a spiritual body', which Bultmann thought was 'not only irrational but completely meaningless'.[30] However, Bultmann was not only a university teacher but also a Lutheran pastor with a very high understanding of the value of preaching. From his pastoral experience he was well aware of the transforming effect on human lives that the preaching of the Gospel can have. He therefore came to the conclusion that the true meaning of the Resurrection should be seen in the fruit its proclamation can bring in the changed lives of faithful Christians today.

In one sense there is much to be said for this perspective, for the New Testament does place considerable weight on the existential consequences of belief in the Resurrection of Christ. St Paul often uses the imagery of resurrection to describe the new quality of life which should be present in the believer through the power of the indwelling and Risen Christ.[31] Paul also draws a direct analogy between the literal death and Resurrection of Jesus and the metaphorical death to sin, and rising up to righteousness, which should follow incorporation into Christ in baptism.[32] But it must be stressed that Paul sees these consequences as entirely dependent on a prior belief in the factual reality of the resurrection of the dead in general and of Jesus in particular: 'if Christ was not raised, then our Gospel is null and void. . . . For if the dead are not raised it follows that Christ was not raised; and if Christ was not raised, your faith has nothing in it and you are still in your old state of sin.'[33] Hence St Paul takes for granted that the existential behavioural changes he observed among the first generation of Christians flowed from their coming to believe in a risen Lord and an eternal destiny. From a New Testament perspective changed lives might be an implication of *belief* in the Resurrection. They cannot be validly described as the *meaning* of the Resurrection.

Resurrection as continuing Jesus' cause

Willi Marxsen argues that the meaning of the Resurrection appearances of Jesus was not to assure the disciples that Jesus had conquered death, but rather to inspire them to carry on with his work. 'The function brought into being by the vision is that the purpose of Jesus is to be continued. What is at stake is that Jesus' kerygma continues to be preached.'[34] Similarly, the Church is described by Paul as the body of Christ, and there is a real sense in which it is called to continue Christ's work. Indeed, every Christian is challenged to embody in his or her life the values Christ taught and practised. As St Teresa put it, 'Christ has no body now on earth but yours. . . . Yours are the eyes through which to look out Christ's compassion to the world. . . . Yours are the hands with which he is to bless men now.'[35] But does this mean that the Resurrection should be identified with the continuation of his work in the Christian community he founded and inspired? Is H.J. Richards right to suggest that the resurrection body is 'nothing other than the church'?[36] Should we join Peter Selby in seeing the basic meaning of the Resurrection as a way of describing the corporate experience of the Christian community?[37] In one sense, all these questions require a positive answer, for they are indeed part of what Resurrection faith is all about. But Christians have always wished to affirm that the Resurrection of Christ meant more than all this. In particular, the first generation of Christians explicitly saw themselves as doing something other than continuing to keep alive the vision, spirit, work and cause of their deceased founder, or simply attempting to follow in the pattern of his life.

In his work *Perestroika* Mikhail Gorbachev writes of the importance of 'turning to Lenin . . . as an inexhaustible source . . . of creative thought and political sagacity. . . . His very image is an undying example of lofty moral strength, all-round spiritual culture, and selfless devotion . . . Lenin lives on in the hearts and minds of millions of people.'[38] I

35

suggest that here we have an instructive parallel to Marxsen's view of Jesus' Resurrection. In the case of Gorbachev there can be little doubt that when he refers to Lenin as 'living on', he means it in an entirely metaphorical sense, as a way of talking about the abiding influence of Lenin's life and teaching, and the continuation of this is the corporate life of the Communist community which he founded. But what is striking about the Epistles of the New Testament is their lack of concern with Jesus' life and teaching. It is remarkable how little can be recovered from the Epistles about what Jesus said and did, and this pattern was continued in the early Church where the whole of Jesus' ministry was summed up in a comma by the historic creeds. Instead of 'continuing Jesus' cause', the first Christians embarked on a wholly new task, namely the proclamation of a message of Jesus' conquest of death and the consequent good news of eternal life after death. This was the message of the first Christians, and this was the centre of Christian preaching throughout the Christian centuries.[39] It is false to the history of the early Church and to the development of Christian doctrine to suggest otherwise.

Conclusion

What I have argued for in this chapter is that the primary meaning of the Resurrection, both in the New Testament and in the historic faith of the Christian Churches, was that Jesus had risen from the dead and brought into being a sense of certainty about a life after death. That message can be interpreted in different ways, because the New Testament itself shows a variety of diverse understandings about how precisely Jesus' conquest of death should be understood. But I have argued that any interpretation which is to do justice to the original message of the Resurrection must talk in terms of belief in life after death for Jesus and for ourselves. This Resurrection faith should bring about consequential changes in our attitudes to life, should unite Christians together in the fellowship of the Church, and should lead to a wish to follow the pattern of Jesus' life.

THE MEANING OF THE RESURRECTION OF JESUS

However, these consequential changes are implications of Resurrection belief, and should not be confused with what the concept of resurrection itself actually means.

Notes

1. Collated from Rufinus, *Apostles' Creed*, para. 42; Revelation 20:13; Augustine, *City of God*, 22.20; Rufinus, para. 43.
2. M.E. Dahl, *The Resurrection of the Body* (London: SCM, 1962), p. 37; John of Damascus, *Exact Exposition*, 4.27.
3. Matthew 28:6; Mark 16:6; Luke 24:3; John 20:7.
4. John 20:17, 20:27.
5. Acts 1:9–11. (Many ancient texts of the New Testament insert a comparably explicit statement into Luke 24:51, and such a view also appears in the longer ending of Mark's Gospel.)
6. For detailed references, see Paul Badham, *Christian Beliefs about Life after Death* (London: SPCK, 1978), p. 155 n. 72.
7. Alan Richardson, *Religion in Contemporary Debate* (London: SCM, 1966), p. 73.
8. For detailed references, see Paul Badham, op. cit., Chapter 3.
9. C.F.D. Moule, *The Significance of the Message of the Resurrection for Faith in Jesus Christ* (London: SCM, 1968), p. 118.
10. Luke 24:31, 24:36; John 20:19, 20:26.
11. John 20:28; Matthew 28:17.
12. Mark 5:41; Luke 7:16; John 11:44.
13. 1 Corinthians 15:55.
14. House of Bishops, *The Nature of Christian Belief* (London: Church House Publishing, 1986), p. 22.
15. Don Cupitt, *Christ and the Hiddenness of God* (Cambridge: Lutterworth, 1971), p. 144.
16. House of Bishops, op. cit., pp. 24–5.
17. 1 Corinthians 15:50, 6:13.
18. 1 Corinthians 15:3–8.
19. Acts 9:3–8, 22:6–11, 26:12–15.
20. Galatians 1:16.
21. Acts 26:19; 1 Corinthians 15:8. (The citation from Acts is from a speech attributed to Paul by Luke and can therefore be used only as supplementary evidence.)
22. For detailed discussion and citation of authorities on this, see Peter Carnley, *The Structure of Resurrection Belief* (Oxford: Clarendon Press, 1987), pp. 206–34.
23. 1 Corinthians 15:36.
24. 1 Corinthians 15:42–4.
25. Acts 26:19.
26. 1 Corinthians 15:44.

27. 1 Peter 3:18.
28. *Doctrine in the Church of England*, p. 209.
29. 2 Corinthians 5:3–4. I take the expression 'inner nature' from the Revised Standard Version translation of 4:16. The Greek text literally means 'the inward of us'.
30. R. Bultmann, 'New Testament and Mythology' in H.W. Bartsch (ed.), *Kerygma and Myth* (New York: Harper & Row, 1961), p. 39 and p. 8.
31. Romans 8:10–11.
32. Romans 6:11; Colossians 2:12–30, 3:1ff.
33. 1 Corinthians 15:15–17.
34. Willi Marxsen, 'The Resurrection of Jesus as a Historical and Theological Problem', in C.F.D. Moule, op. cit.
35. Cited in Normal Bull, *A Book of School Worship* (London: Harrap, 1965), p. 21.
36. H.J. Richards, *Death and After* (London: Fount, 1980), pp. 38–9.
37. Peter Selby, *Look for the Living: the Corporate Nature of Resurrection Faith* (London: SCM, 1976), Chapter 6.
38. Mikhail Gorbachev, *Perestroika* (New York: Harper & Row, 1987), p. 25.
39. Paul Badham, op. cit., Chapters 2 and 3.

3. The Four Gospels: Four Perspectives on the Resurrection*

John Fenton

The problem

The final chapters of the four Gospels are so similar and yet so different that it is difficult to remember the content of any one of them accurately. Sample test questions would be: How many women went to see the tomb in Matthew's account? How many angels did they see in Mark's? Which Evangelist refers to an appearance to Peter? In which Gospel is the appearance to Thomas? The nineteenth-century writer Samuel Butler, with his unerring instinct for disclosing embarrassing situations, makes good use of the problem that the endings of the Gospels create when he has Mr Shaw, the tinker, ask Ernest Pontifex, the curate, in *The Way of All Flesh* (probably written in 1867 but not published until 1903), to give him 'the story of the Resurrection of Jesus Christ as told in St John's Gospel'; the reader can only sympathise with Ernest as he confuses John with Matthew.

The curate consults the works of Dean Alford (1810–71) but finds no help there. Alford took the view that none of the Evangelists had access to the Gospels of the others, but each depended on the oral tradition that had been established by the Apostles themselves. On this way of understanding the Gospels, the differences between them were almost inexplicable, and this is what Ernest realised:

When he had finished Dean Alford's notes he found them come

* © John Fenton 1993

to this, namely, that no one yet had succeeded in bringing the four accounts into tolerable harmony with each other, and that the Dean, seeing no chance of succeeding better than his predecessors had done, recommended that the whole story should be taken on trust – and this Ernest was not prepared to do.

Had the novel been written a century later, Ernest Pontifex need not have been as devastated as Butler imagined. At the very least he could have had a method of relating the four accounts to one another that would have made it easier to remember what each Evangelist said; but he might also have been able to see why they differed from each other and how it had to be so.

Biblical criticism

The way in which biblical criticism has developed in the last hundred years or so has produced positive results. It is not the case that it has been only destructive. The patient and painstaking work of scholars has made it possible for us to understand these ancient texts in such a way as to allow them to bear witness to the faith of their authors in the Resurrection of Christ and to invite us to share this faith with them. What had been a stumbling-block has become a sign, and what had been a problem is now a bonus.

Two insights in particular have contributed to this new situation in which we can now read the last chapters of the Gospels and find them creative and productive of faith. The first of these is the realisation that Mark is the source used by Matthew and Luke. The other is the suggestion that the original ending of Mark's Gospel was at the point when the women fled from the tomb and said nothing to anyone because they were afraid; that not only did Mark stop there but that he intended to stop there; that was where the copies of Mark used by Matthew and Luke also stopped, and anything that was added was added later.

With these two insights, the reader of Matthew can now see that all that is not from Mark is an addition to an earlier and shorter account; and it is not difficult to see why such additions might have been felt to be necessary. Similarly Luke, on this understanding, has revised Mark in certain ways and added further narratives of Resurrection appearances that link his first volume to his second (the Acts of the Apostles) by preparing for the preaching of the disciples. This leaves us with the Fourth Gospel; does the priority of Mark help us to explain the last two chapters of John? Not as directly and obviously as in the case of the other two gospels, but it may help us, nevertheless. There was no account of an appearance of the risen Christ in Mark, but there are such accounts in John; on the other hand, we are now told that those who have believed without seeing are blessed. What John gives, he also takes away; and in this respect he may be, as has been claimed, our best guide to understanding Mark; there too, in the body of the Gospel, what was given was immediately withdrawn, by means of the commands to silence.

The problem raised by the last chapters of the Gospels is not a historical problem (What actually happened on Easter Day?) but a literary problem (Why do the Evangelists write in different ways?) – this is the direction in which twentieth-century study of the Gospels has pointed us. The appropriate way to solve the problem is not by asking historical questions: Who went to the tomb? Who saw what? Who said what to whom?, but by asking questions to do with authors: Why does this Evangelist tell the story in this way? Why does he alter what was in his source? Why does he add this or that new incident? What we have is Scripture; texts, not events. Strictly speaking, we do not even have Evangelists, though we may sometimes think we know them and their intentions, and may be wrong to do so. We have texts that are there to be read and pondered with the aid of whatever help we can find.

Four perspectives

Mark

The three women in Mark's account stand in for the disciples who have all run away; we met them at the end of the description of the Crucifixion watching from a distance.

41

They call to mind a passage in the Greek translation of one of the Psalms:

> My friends and my neighbours came near and stood opposite me, and my kinsfolk stood at a distance (Psalm 38:11; in Greek, Psalm 37:12).

One of the women, Mark says, was Mary the mother of James and Joses; and he had told us already that these were the names of two of the brothers of Jesus and that his mother was Mary. The Psalm leads us to think that the women have not understood Jesus any more than the men; and this is confirmed by their coming to anoint the body on the first day of the week; they have not believed his repeated prediction that he would rise again after three days, and his assertion that his body had already been anointed for burial. Their conversation, moreover, confirms our expectations: they discuss who will remove the stone from the door of the tomb; but it has already been removed. They were wrong about the stone, and they will be wrong also about the body. Mark tells the whole story with extreme restraint and under-statement. There are no angels in his account, only a young man wearing a white garment. He rebukes the women: they should not be seeking Jesus, the man from Nazareth, the one who was crucified, because he is not here, but risen. They are invited to see the empty space where he had been put, but (unlike John) Mark does not say that they looked at what there was to be seen. There is no attention in this account to the circumstances of the Resurrection or to the evidence for it provided by the disappearance of the body or the state of the grave cloths. Mark draws our attention to two things instead: one is the message that is to be given to the disciples and Peter: they will see Jesus, as he had said, in Galilee. The other is that the story ends, as it began, in failure to believe, and fear.

The words of the young man, 'As he told you', refer us back to the two places in this Gospel where Jesus spoke about his being seen: 'Then they will see the Son of Man coming in the clouds with great power and glory' (Mark 13:26), and 'You will see the Son of Man seated at the right hand of God and coming with the clouds of heaven' (Mark 14:62). Mark's Gospel ends where it began: it started with the promise that the kingdom of God was at hand; it ends with the same assurance. The book is good news about God, that he is going to reign; so it can only stop, like the final speech of Jesus, by pointing forward to what is to come next: 'What I say to you, I say to everyone: keep awake' (Mark 13:37).

This unwillingness to allow the reader's attention to concentrate on the intermediate and penultimate has been a characteristic of Mark's Gospel throughout. We find it in the repeated conjunction 'and immediately' which gives his narrative a sense of movement and urgency; there is no time to dally, and even when they attempt to rest, they cannot (Mark 6:30ff). We find it also in the commands to silence which are such a well-known feature of this book; one explanation of them is that Mark does not want his readers to pause and wonder at the miracles of healing but to move on to the greater event of the death, Resurrection and coming in glory. Whatever his reason, he does not allow us to see Jesus again on the page of his text, between the burial of the corpse and his coming in the clouds. The Resurrection after three days is the promise of the new age, and to live by faith is to live in hope.

The silence of the women is an act of disobedience: they were commanded by the 'omniscient' young man to speak, but they did not do so; they fled, and they were silent. Both verbs are followed by an explanatory clause, each introduced by the word 'for'. Trembling, amazement and fear were the cause of their disobedience and, as Mark sees it, this is the opposite of faith: 'Do not fear, only believe' (Mark 5:36).

If this is where the original author ended his Gospel, then we know that two later writers found the book inadequate (perhaps because they were then in a position to compare Mark with other Gospels which had raised their expectations of further narratives). These two later writers were the authors of the longer ending of Mark and the shorter. If Mark was used by Matthew, Luke and John, then here were three other writers who were dissatisfied with what they found in the earlier Gospel and wrote to supply what they felt

43

was needed. Mark is therefore 'responsible' for the writing of the other accounts, in the sense that he did not satisfy the needs of all his readers; he created a vacuum which others filled. What these needs were, we can discover by reading the other Gospels.

Matthew

Almost all of the final paragraph in Mark is present in the last chapter of Matthew, and much else beside. Absent is the discussion about rolling away the stone, because we are told in this Gospel that the stone had been sealed and a guard placed to prevent anyone from entering the tomb. For the same reason, there is no mention of anointing the body; the women are coming only to see the tomb. We saw how in Mark women stand in for the disciples, and both groups are failures; this is not so in Matthew: the disciples are called 'blessed', and the women are obedient.

Among the new elements in Matthew's account are the earthquake, the descent of the angel of the Lord who takes the place of the young man in Mark and rolls away the stone and sits on it, and the terror of the guards. But the most significant addition is the result of the change he has made in the description of the women. In Matthew, fear can mean good and holy reverence, whereas in Mark it was always an unbelieving reaction to revelation. The women's fear in Matthew is compatible with great joy and they run (not flee) to obey the angel's command and tell the disciples. But lest Mark should have left us in doubt about the ability of the women to act upon the message of the angel of the Lord, Jesus himself appears to them, they grasp his feet and worship him, and Jesus repeats what the angel had said, calling his disciples his brothers. Then Matthew completes his story of the guard, and of the deliberate deceit of the Sanhedrin, and so brings his readers to the final scene in Galilee where Jesus sends his disciples to the Gentiles.

Matthew provides not only the answers to the questions that Mark had raised but also (explicitly or by implication) the questions to which they were the answers: Who rolled away the stone? The angel of the Lord did it. Could Jesus be seen and touched after the Resurrection? Yes, the women clasped his feet. Why were the disciples to go to Galilee? In order to receive the final words of Jesus, and go from there to the Gentiles. Where is Jesus, until he comes to judge the world? He is with us all the days, till that day comes. Why was the tomb empty? Not because the disciples removed the body, as the Jews continued to say; they could not have done so, because of the guard, and the story that the guard was asleep was fabricated by the Sanhedrin itself to protect them from the truth of the matter which would have been so fatal.

The history that has given rise to Matthew's alterations to his source is the history of the Church and the Jews in the latter half of the first century, not the events of Easter Day. We notice the shift from the future to the present: Jesus has received all authority, and he acts authoritatively in sending his disciples to baptise and to teach; they do not live by the hope of his coming but by the faith that he is present. The Church is filling the vacuum that Mark's book created: we have an authoritative teacher, his laws to keep, and his Church to belong to, and he is with us till the end.

Luke
Whereas Mark and Matthew had been writing conclusions to their books, Luke composed what is only the ending of the first part of his two-volume work. His purpose here, there-fore, is to produce a passage that will act as a bridge between the ministry of Jesus in Galilee, Samaria and Jerusalem, and the preaching of his followers in Jerusalem, Judaea, Samaria and to the ends of the earth. This explains why he changes Mark's reference to Galilee as the place to which the dis-ciples must go to see him (when he comes in glory), into Galilee as the place where Jesus had foretold his Crucifixion and Resurrection; the coming in glory is less prominent in Luke than it is in Mark. As in Matthew, which Luke may have known, the women obey the command, though the disciples do not believe them. Luke then has the long and continuous narrative of the appearance to two of the followers on the way to Emmaus, their return to Jerusalem, the information that the Lord has already appeared to Simon, and the final

appearance, as it seems, in Jerusalem. Luke, again like Matthew, has the command to preach to all the nations, but, unlike Matthew, this is to be done first in Jerusalem. In two further respects Luke agrees with Matthew. First, the Resurrection body was no ghost; Matthew had said that the women grasped his feet; Luke tells us that he ate broiled fish. Secondly, Jesus was the fulfilment of the Law, the Prophets and the Psalms: he said so himself.

The events contained in this final chapter of Luke can scarcely be historical as they stand: evening was drawing on when they reached Emmaus; Cleopas and his companion must return the seven miles to Jerusalem; then there is the appearance to all the disciples and the walk to Bethany, before Jesus is parted from them and they return to Jerusalem and the temple. Just as this final day seems to be a Lucan device (which it is hard to reconcile with the statement in Acts that Jesus appeared over a period of forty days), so also the events of the day may well be a Lucan creation for which he need have had no sources other than Mark, the tradition that Jesus appeared first to Simon, faith in the reality of the Resurrection, and the pattern of promise and fulfilment to which he refers frequently in the speeches in Acts.

There is a further small but significant point of contact between Luke and Matthew: in Matthew, the chief priests and the Pharisees say to Pilate, 'Sir, we remember that that deceiver said, while he was still alive (*eti zōn*), "After three days I shall be raised up" ' (Matthew 27:63). It is a statement made by unbelievers, and it is the only place in the New Testament where the verb 'to live' (*zēn*) is used with reference to Jesus of the time before the Resurrection; the usual order of words is to say that he died and lives, not that he lived and died; his life began on Easter Day. Moreover, Matthew's faith is that Jesus continues to remain with his disciples till the end of the age. But Luke's emphasis is different from Matthew's: Luke will develop the idea of the Holy Spirit as the power and inspiration of the disciples from Pentecost onwards. Jesus himself ascends to God's right hand, and Luke is the only New Testament writer who separates this from Easter and ascribes it to a particular day, forty days after. It is only in Luke that Jesus speaks of the time past as the time 'when I was still with you' (*eti ōn sun humin*, Luke 24:44; see also verse 6); he ascends to heaven in the body of flesh and bone in which he had appeared and in which he had eaten with them. In Luke, the presence of Jesus is a thing of the past, just as it was to the chief priests and Pharisees in Matthew. What matters to Luke is the presence of the Holy Spirit; and in order to receive this gift, there must be contact with the Church in Jerusalem through the Apostles or those delegated by them. We are on the way towards a doctrine of apostolic succession and the primacy of one particular Church.

John

The final chapters of John (20 and 21) bear a different relationship to the rest of his Gospel from the relationship of the final chapters of the other three Gospels to the main part of their books. This is so because the Resurrection means something different to John from what it meant to the other Evangelists: to them, it was God's reversal of what was done to Jesus on Good Friday; to John, it is the way in which certain people came to faith.

It has often been pointed out that John had no need to tell Resurrection stories; his book had already reached its climax long before this. But, perhaps as a concession to tradition, he continues the narrative in order to tell us how faith began. He therefore has to shift the point of view from which the stories are now told. During the long speeches at the supper, the reader had come to understand faith from the point of view of Jesus, the speaker and himself the object of faith: 'Believe in God, believe also in me' (John 14:1). John does not attempt to describe the Resurrection through the eyes of Jesus, but he invites us by his stories to identify ourselves with Mary Magdalene, Peter, the disciple whom Jesus loved, and Thomas. He continues to use the device he had so frequently employed in the earlier part of his book, that of misunderstanding followed by realisation of the truth.

Thus Mary Magdalene is brought by the voice of Jesus,

who calls her by name, from the error of thinking that there has been a theft of the body (cf. Matthew) through an intermediate relationship expressed by the term *Rabbuni*, 'Master', which had been appropriate in the past, to a new kind of union with Jesus in the Father. The disciples, too, are brought from fear of the Jews to peace, and are given the Spirit and their mission that will bring forgiveness and judgement to the world. Thomas is offered proof, but is told that those who believe without it will be blessed; and this leads into what seems to have been the original end of the Gospel – the book was written to make faith, life and blessedness a possibility for those who did not see.

The final chapter seems to be an appendix, though whether it was added by the author of Chapters 1–20 or by another writer is uncertain. Nor is it altogether clear what need or purpose was served by the additional material. Again the story is told from the point of view of the disciples: the night of taking no fish is followed by the morning catch in obedience to the Lord; they eat with him (cf. Luke); Peter is commanded to be the pastor of the flock and his martyrdom is foretold; and a misunderstanding about the disciple whom Jesus loved is corrected. Finally, here and only here in the Fourth Gospel, it is said that this disciple is the author, presumably of the whole book, not just of Chapter 21.

The reader of this final chapter suspects he is overhearing the conflicts and tensions within the Churches at the time of the writing of the Fourth Gospel, and that he does not know enough about the situation to be able to make complete sense of what is being said. The rivalry between Peter and the disciple whom Jesus loved is involved, and this may point to the difference between this Gospel and the other three (in which Peter's primacy is acknowledged). Was the chapter added in order to commend this strange Gospel to Churches that had previously accepted only one or more of the other three? If that were the reason for the adding of Chapter 21 to a previously complete book, we should have a further example of how Resurrection narratives in the Gospels are to be read as the conclusions to the books they are in: they are attempts to deal with the practical problem that faced every Evangelist, How shall I finish off a book that is about an eternal gospel? (Revelation 14:6).

Conclusion

The four Evangelists describe Easter Day in four different ways, because the books they are writing are different from each other. It has been said that, 'It is one of the great charms of books that they have to end' (F. Kermode, *The Sense of an Ending* (1966), p. 23). They can only end in the way that their authors dictate that they should. Matthew could not adopt Mark's ending without altering it and adding to it, nor could Luke take over either Mark's or Matthew's; none of the previous accounts of the finding of the empty tomb or of the appearances of the Lord after the Resurrection was satisfactory to John. Each Evangelist had his own way of telling the story, in accordance with his perception of the faith.

A very rough and ready guide to the Resurrection stories in the four Gospels is to imagine that each of the Evangelists is engaged in answering the question, Where is Jesus now? Mark's answer is: He is coming soon; be ready and stay awake. Matthew's is: He is Emmanuel, God with us when we meet in his name; he continues to proclaim the coming kingdom, to teach us and to heal us, and to be our ransom. Luke's answer to the question is: He is at God's right hand in heaven, pouring forth the Spirit so that we can preach repentance and forgiveness of sins in his name. To John, the answer is: He is in us and we are in him, through the Spirit he has breathed upon us. The Easter stories are expressions of the Easter faith; that is the way they should be read.

Further reading

Evans, C.F., *Resurrection and the New Testament* (London: SCM Press, 1970)

Houlden, J.L., *Backward into Light* (London: SCM, 1987)

Lightfoot, R.H., *Locality and Doctrine* (London: Hodder & Stoughton, 1938)

Marxsen, W., *The Resurrection of Jesus of Nazareth* (London: SCM, 1970)

Perrin, N., *The Resurrection according to Matthew, Mark and Luke* (Philadelphia: Fortress Press, 1977)

4. The Resurrection:
History, Story and Belief*

Leslie Houlden

In 1911, Charles Gore was made Bishop of Oxford and was required to inhabit the Palace at Cuddesdon in the Oxfordshire countryside. Unfashionably for his time, and perhaps for any time, he demurred. He felt an incongruity between the Christian ministry and palatial life. There was nothing suprising in his adopting this attitude: more than twenty years before, he had established himself as one of the leaders of the second wave of Christian social theology in the Church of England, following the work of F.D. Maurice, J.M. Ludlow and others in the 1840s. As an undergraduate at Oxford, Gore had come under the influence of T.H. Green, not only in philosophy, but more in the social application of Christianity. He was one of the first leaders of the Christian Social Union when it was founded in 1889. He was also the leading founder of the Community of the Resurrection among whose ideals was the renewal of Christian witness in the industrial wasteland, expressed in the Community's settling of its headquarters at Mirfield in the West Riding of Yorkshire. Gore had underpinned his 'bias to the poor' theologically in his contribution to *Lux Mundi* in 1889 and his Bampton Lectures on Christology two years later. Squalor and poverty in human society, far from being the opportunity for divine blessing, were an affront to the God who had sanctified society by his incarnate presence: as the homiletic epigram put it (strikingly within a setting Catholic in thought and piety), a slum is as

* © Leslie Houlden 1988, 1993

much an insult to the God we worship as a filthy chalice at the Eucharist.

Already on his appointment to the see of Worcester in 1902, Gore had tried without success to avoid living in the house of the see, Hartlebury Castle, for nobody could quite see a way of enabling him to achieve this little piece of integrity. But in 1911 he tried again, and formed the plan of giving over the Palace at Cuddesdon to the work of training poor young men for the ministry. It was a breed then scarcely to be found in the Church of England, though it was encouraged to some degree in the work of the Theological Department at King's College, London, with part-time evening courses, established temporarily in 1908, which enabled men to scrape a living and study at the same time. (There had been a few other moves in the same direction, including the setting up of a theological college at Mirfield itself.)

Gore consulted about his project with his friend and a successor of his as Principal of Pusey House in Oxford, Stuckey Coles, now remembered for a brace of hymns of a modestly poetic quality and another best forgotten. The Dictionary of National Biography notes concerning him, on the one hand, the 'great spiritual beauty' of his face, and on the other about the three difficulties that beset him: being excessively stout, being bad at games, and being too high church. When I first read Coles's reply to Gore's letter, which fell from between the pages of a book, I experienced a considerable socio-theological shock.

There had been a theological college at Cuddesdon, immediately opposite the episcopal house, for nearly sixty years. There, as for another half-century, an almost exclusively Oxbridge, almost exclusively public school group of ordinands was trained (or at any rate prepared) for the ministry. In placing so near to the college a new group which, socially, was so far removed, Coles saw danger. What struck him was not that the poor men might feel embarrassed at the near presence of their well-off social betters across the road, but that the better-off would feel discomfort at the proximity of their social inferiors – men destined for the same ministry but with no expectation of ever obtain-

51

ing the professional plums of their future career. Our upper-class ordinands, he was clear, could not deal with this manifestation of the poor, and must not be prematurely and so ambiguously brought into touch with the class to which they would soon devote their pastoral efforts. Later, but not now, the ideals of both priesthood and accustomed social order would be achieved harmoniously and simultaneously. Meanwhile, dissonance had better be avoided.

Just to complete the tale: Gore's plan never came off, and he remained in his palace with a dozen servants, including two coachmen – this despite the fact that by then there was no coach but a single motor-car. By 1912, Coles was installed as his chaplain and trusted friend. Gore remained in the see until in 1919 he could stand church business no longer and became for the last decade of his life a theology lecturer at King's College, London, and was eventually in charge of post-graduate students in theology. He thus contributed to the work in which Coles and others had frustrated him.

My aim in recounting this episode is not to evoke either applause for Gore's laudable plan, or amazed contempt for Coles's reaction (though I should not mind if you felt either), but to point to important choices in theological method. Here were two men, Coles and Gore, not dissimilar in social background and formation; both, that is, from the upper end of the scale. They were similar too in theological outlook: both belonged to the third generation of the Catholic revival in the Church of England which the Oxford Movement had initiated in the 1830s. Both held to the fore certain beliefs about the Church, the Eucharist, and the ministry. The careers of both had moved among the offices one might expect. Gore had gone from the chaplaincy of Trinity College, Oxford, to be the first Principal of Pusey House, established in the Catholic interest, in the face of a predicted tide of secularism which would, it was feared, finally sweep the Church out of the University altogether. Coles had also served on the staff of Pusey House and been its Principal for three years.

Yet here was this cleavage of outlook on a matter of policy and, behind that, on social propriety in the light of Christian belief: to live in a palace or to found a college, to maintain the established order or to meet the Church's need and enable men of modest social background to fulfil a vocation to the priesthood. How are we to evaluate this division? If we make a comparison of the two men's views, do we count them as at one on almost everything, and see this merely as a difference of view about a scheme which one might or might not fulfil? Or is there here a symptom which points to two utterly different theological worlds? Is it perhaps a small door which opens immediately on to two paths, between which one must choose – two paths leading to two quite different pictures of Christian truth as a whole?

To put it in another way: is a person's mind fairly and usefully revealed in his or her admitted beliefs and opinions, or are we to take account of the totality of the person's life, with every aspect of it legitimately contributing to our picture and our assessment? In another analogy: I listen to an aria from *The Marriage of Figaro*, and I am moved by its sublimity. I turn to the words and find them banal in the extreme. Do I note the incongruity and leave it at that? Or do I observe that Mozart has got it absolutely right: beneath even our humdrum situations and our comments on them, there is always the abyss of human potential for triumph or for tragedy? It may then be that, whatever the causes they espoused together, Gore and Coles were poles apart, their respective theological worlds disclosed by their perception of the college for poor ordinands in relation to the rich men across the road. By such a symptom we may see a difference of understanding of God and of Christian faith which goes to the very roots.

Supposing that one adopts such an approach in understanding and assessing the theology of a person, a group, or even a period, then certainly one is working in a manner which, if not at all unheard of, is scarcely digested in any quarters at all. It is a manner of perception which is a first fruit of that style of theology distinguished now, ill definedly but helpfully and even necessarily, by the term 'narrative'. It is marked by its attention to story-line, movement, development and structure in the expression of theological ideas, whether in books or in lives; and in those aspects meaning is to be found. As far as the theological discipline is concerned (for its original habitat is partly in anthropology, partly in literary criticism), it has nowhere had more fruitful exploitation than in relation to the Gospels. By contrast with the historical orientation of the various critical methods of the past and much of the present, here now is a way of looking at the Gospels, which, with increasing subtlety and ingenuity, leaves all that aside and investigates the text as text: Gospels not as collections of traditional material, not as reflecting early Church situations and needs, or as recording episodes in the life of Jesus, but as words on pages, compositions, wholes, with beginnings, endings, frameworks and structures. There is to my mind often too great a rigour in critical works of this kind in excluding concern with the historical location of the work, especially with regard to the mind and purpose of the Gospel author. And if in the end rounded, comprehensive understanding is what one is after, then it is hard to see that one can leave aside an interest in the author's setting. Behind texts are minds, and minds exist in humans, who live in society and do many other things besides write texts – in a welter of activities which affect each other, each one having its bearing on the rest.

So the usefulness of attention to the text as text may finally be to bring about awareness of one aspect of the reality concerning the writing: one aspect among others, but one hitherto neglected or underplayed. Sometimes it will command the reconsideration of judgements brought about by other approaches. For example, a 'narrative' reading of the Gospel of Mark, making us aware of the complex counterpoint of the text, forces upon us a view of the author, and perhaps the Christian group which presumably found his work intelligible, which is far removed from many customary accounts of those matters. This writer was no simple collector of tales and sayings of Jesus, no naïve apocalyptic sectary; nor was his church community merely a group of simple persons agape at the marvels done by Jesus and longing for his return. There is instead extreme subtlety of reference and interconnection, giving a multi-dimensional confrontation with Jesus who remains a figure of infinitive mysteriousness. Moreover, it is the narrative reading which can claim the greatest objectivity: it is an interpretation confined to what is there, the text; while all historical reconstruction is, however intelligent, largely hypothetical, so little remains that can take us reliably behind the text.

The Synoptic Gospels in particular, with their blend of similarity and difference, afford endless opportunities to pursue the method of opening small doors that lead to large and alternative worlds. Let us grasp just one such opportunity. It is afforded by the final chapters of the two Gospels of Mark and Luke.

By the time we reach the end of Chapter 15 of Mark, with its account of Jesus' burial, he has already told us four times that, despite the overwhelming weight of the Passion story, the tale will not end there. There have been three omnibus prophecies by Jesus of coming betrayal, death and resurrection; and shortly before the betrayal, there was the more enigmatic statement: 'It is written, "I will strike the shepherd, and the sheep will be scattered". But after I am raised up, I will go before you into Galilee.'

But now, when only resurrection remains to tell, there is what can only be called at first sight, in terms of the story, the most severe anticlimax: a mere eight verses of writing, no appearance of Jesus, only a tomb empty and the testimony that 'he has been raised, he is not here' given by an unnamed young man, mysteriously reminiscent of the young man in Gethsemane, who first 'followed' and then 'fled'. Mark pointed up the reminiscence by using for Jesus' shroud the same word that he had used for the young man's abandoned garment. The anticlimax is intensified by the confusion of the women who came to anoint the corpse. They came to the tomb all right, but only on arrival did they note the difficulty, in fact removed, of shifting the stone from the tomb's mouth. But the message of resurrection they received with no joy, only fear and amazement, and having been instructed to give out the message, 'they said nothing to anyone, for they were afraid'.

The story seemed, of course, so unsatisfactory that people were unable to leave it as it was. Whatever it was intended to convey was either misunderstood or, if understood, found intolerable. Matthew and Luke, both using it fully in their later Gospels, retold it, removing the disturbing features we have noted and substituting certainty for enigma. People react with joy; the women report as bidden; authoritative angels replace the young man without credentials; and above all, Jesus himself appears. Matthew and Luke were Mark's first interpreters, and a warning to all interpreters how easily they can mistake the meaning of their text, as they determine to make their own sense of it. Later still, at least two unknown writers added pieces to Mark's Gospel itself, with the same objective: no book about Jesus, the centre of faith, could be left as Mark had left his book.

Luke's reworking of Mark's story goes further than his careful and minute doctoring of those eight inherited verses. Now, they have become merely the opening episode of a Resurrection chapter in four sections; first, the tomb; then the walk to Emmaus; then a scene with the disciples in Jerusalem; and finally a parting at Bethany. It is possible, common, but in the end idle, to speculate on the source of these further elements. They have their affinities with stories found elsewhere, especially in John, but as they stand (and it is especially true of the Emmaus story) they are Luke's work, Luke's offering, and we read his text. We cannot tell whether his idea was simply to add more stories, filling out Mark's minimal tale, proceeding like a collector, a chronicler. What we can describe is the effect on ourselves. The Emmaus story – the walk, the conversation, and above all the meal – dominates the account. Whether we think of Luke's first readers or ourselves, his umpteenth readers, that story falls into place as one of many in Luke–Acts, where meals with Jesus or in imitation of such meals form the scene. This is, however, the most striking of them all, a kind of paradigm. It is a narrative of religious recognition, here in Eucharistic fellowship; of faith rekindled in such fellowship; of Jesus' story as fulfilling ancient and basic scriptures; and of Jerusalem as the centre for such fulfilment.

This last feature, the heart of Luke's theological geography, is the most striking and pervasive aspect of his reworking of Mark. For Mark, the message at the tomb pointed to Galilee: 'he goes before you into Galilee – there you will see him'. There is no hint as to what that might mean: is it about the literal Galilee as the continuing centre of the Jesus movement, or a hint of the location of Mark's own community? Or is it symbolic – but then, symbolic of what? Of the mission transcending frontiers and looking always beyond? Of Jesus' eventual return? Of limitless, faith-demanding horizons? There is really no clarity: the answer lies perhaps in some kind of code or private language of the Marcan community. Whatever it was, Luke told the story otherwise, with Jerusalem as the source and base for Christian life and activity: it is part of a whole Lucan doctrine, already established in the birth stories, of Jesus, and what stems from him, as springing from yet superseding the Judaism of which Jerusalem and its temple were the symbol.

Moreover, whereas for Mark the story in his final chapter is his conclusion, however strange it may be in that role, Luke's Resurrection story looks still further ahead – to Jesus' removal to heaven, his 'entry into glory', and his heavenly reign, under which the mission described in the Acts of the Apostles takes place. The Resurrection sequence is not the climax, but a stage on the journey; thus Luke adjusts still more the proportion of things, the placing of the weight of belief.

Small doors opening on to alternative worlds. It is, in fact, a case of a multiplicity of doors: almost any episodes shared by the two writers would serve our purpose. The alternative worlds would, however, be the same in all cases, the world of Mark and the world of Luke. They are in the first place alternative worlds of religious sensibility.

In the case of Mark, it is a world of surprise, uncertainty, enigma and a certain passivity. There is surprise at being offered so little, here, above all points, where the grandest of grand finales might be expected. There is uncertainty (assuredly felt by us – whether by the first readers we cannot tell) about what is intended by so many aspects of the story:

57

what or where is Galilee where the disciples will see him? What is the force of 'and Peter' in the words 'Go tell his disciples *and Peter*'? How are we to suppose the news got out if the women 'said nothing to anyone'? Does it cover an awkwardness – that once, the empty tomb was not known about? But in any case, what is the meaning of his dialectic of 'Go tell' and 'they said nothing'? And above all, what kind of an event is this 'being raised' that has happened to Jesus, and what kind of a 'seeing' is it that will take place in Galilee? None of this is elucidated in the least. There is a certain passivity, in the sense that none of the enigma element appears to matter. Mark is wholly devoid of concern to offer proofs or authentication. He is at the opposite extreme from those who seek to explain exactly what occurred, to make a historically satisfactory tale. To the modern reader who is after that kind of knowledge, his advice is bound to seem: 'Relax, you're barking up the wrong tree.'

In the case of Luke, it is a world of warmth and assurance. The warmth is evident in the achieved and recognised presence of Jesus. The men who walked to Emmaus testify to this very feeling: 'Did not our hearts burn within us as he spoke to us on the road?' It is evident in the 'great joy' of the disciples as they return to Jersualem after the parting, with which Luke's Gospel, part one of his work, comes to an end. The assurance is equally clear: in the authority of the two angelic figures who address the women at the tomb; in the reminder they give that Jesus' prophecy of his rising was there to be fulfilled; in the two pointers to Old Testament scriptures, also now fulfilled; in Jesus' reference to his palpable hands and feet, falsifying their suspicion that this is a ghost, and in his as-it-were-brazenly demanding fish to eat. Luke makes it as clear as possible that there is no mystery or puzzle here at all, that surprise is misplaced, that faith is the obvious response and a matter of sheer delight; and that faith rests on certainty.

If these are alternative worlds of religious sensibility, are they also alternative worlds of theology, of serious belief? Like Charles Gore and Stuckey Coles, Mark and Luke have much belief in common. Both can speak of Jesus in the same terms: he is son of God, he is son of man, he is Messiah, his career is all 'according to the scriptures', long purposed by God, and that purpose is due for final fulfilment, centring still on Jesus. But at this point, the 'narrative' approach to these matters asserts itself. First, it erases my distinction between 'religious sensibility' and that term, 'serious belief', with which I patronised it. Those items on which Mark and Luke agree are, of course, significant for certain purposes, like the resolutions with which a contentious meeting concludes; but much more significant and certainly more interesting are the total settings, the whole narrative within which they belong and in which they carry such different meanings. What I put into the box of 'sensibility' is, in fact, itself a mode of theological perception. It is itself a style of response, all the richer for its many, interlocking aspects.

Anyone interested in exploring a narrative approach in theology, and especially with regard to the Gospels as theological documents, should consider taking Clement of Alexandria as whatever is the opposite of a patron saint. For he (at the end of the second century) distinguished between the Gospel of John and the rest. That Gospel, with its apparently superior elaboration of ideas, and depth of religious insight, was the 'spiritual' gospel, fit for those Christians who had reached a certain level of proficiency. The other Gospels were for simple Christians, whose faith could be suitably fed by stories. In at last reversing that trend, concern with narrative and the treasures it may disclose is striking a tardy blow for spiritual and theological democracy.

I referred a moment ago to the many interlocking aspects which emerge in a narrative appreciation of a text. I turn now to another feature of the movement of stories, and this too is of some theological interest. Again I propose to use the Gospel stories as my example. But before moving to the matter of substance, I make one observation about the early development of belief about Jesus' Resurrection. There is in the development something of a paradox. If we trace that belief from our earliest evidence, in the work of Paul the Apostle, on into the second century, we can detect two contrary processes, if we compare the development of the perception of event with the development of belief. In a nutshell, 'event' becomes ever more defined, while belief becomes ever more dispersed.

First, *event*: in Paul, notoriously and maddeningly, the facts of Jesus' Resurrection itself are unclear. Faith is unclouded but, whatever may legitimately be surmised, there is no mention of an empty tomb, no definition of the character of Jesus' risen-ness or of the 'appearances', which are the sole aspect clearly referred to. While, on the one hand, the reference to an appearance, otherwise unknown, to '500 brothers at once' carries an impression of objectivity (though not immune from sceptical attention), on the other hand, Paul's inclusion of his own 'call' experience with the other 'appearances' confuses us. Now, of course, there is no sense in moving from 'Paul did not say' to 'Paul did not know' or even 'Paul did not care' in relation to this or that circumstance; but the fact remains that for us as readers, as testimony to the 'event' moves on from Paul and finds expression in more plainly narrative form, the questions he left unanswered begin to be dealt with. Mark, for all his mysteriousness, presents us with the empty tomb. Matthew strengths the point with the testimony not of a fallible young man but of an angel from heaven, and with the tale about the guard and their being bribed by the authorities. He answers other questions, too. In Mark, the promise of reunion in Galilee was left in the air, unfulfilled, leaving us quite uncertain what kind of fulfilment might be in view. In Matthew, we need only read for a few lines to find it resoundingly fulfilled: 'the eleven disciples went to Galilee to the mountain where Jesus had arranged with them and seeing him they worshipped'. Rendezvous are for keeping. And if Mark had left indeterminate what Jesus' status now was, Matthew leaves no doubt: he is indeed to be worshipped, for 'all authority in heaven and on earth has been given' to him. And what assurance might there be for those not of that first group of followers? That too is provided for: the Gospel ends, 'Behold I am with you all the days, until the end of the age.'

In Luke, more questions still find their answer, more blurs are cleared. Was Jesus' risen body real and solid? Yes, it was, he drew attention to it and he ate fish. What was the nature of his appearances? Well, he appeared in rooms, and then there were partings. John makes many of those same points: Thomas touches him or at least is invited to do so, the wounds are plain, and Jesus cooks by the lakeside. Moreover, the factuality of his rising is demonstrated, not this time by soldiers, but by the disciples' testimony about the layout of the grave-clothes: precisely thus and not otherwise they were arranged. Finally, in the Gospel of Peter, the event of Jesus' rising comes fully before our eyes. '[The soldiers] saw the heavens opened and two men come down from there. . . . That stone which had been laid against the entrance to the tomb started of itself to roll away . . . and both the young men entered in. . . . And while [the soldiers] were relating what they had seen, they saw again three men come out from the tomb, and two of them sustaining the other, and a cross following them, and the heads of the two reaching to heaven, but that of him who was led of them by the hand overpassing the heavens.' The surreal quality of this Resurrection story (and of all the stories it is the one that most merits that name) should not blind us to its role in the development we are tracing. In it, 'happenedness' concerning the Resurrection reaches its climax and virtually its terminus: we have seen all there is to see. It only remained – it waited two more centuries – to set about locating the site of the Resurrection and build a church on it.

It has, of course, long been customary to single out the Gospel of Peter and dismiss its account as legendary; but from the point of view of narrative development, it represents the final clarification, in that sense the moment of truth. The perception of 'event' becomes ever more defined.

Secondly, by contrast, *belief* becomes ever more dispersed. In Paul, belief in the Resurrection is in a state of pristine clarity. In tandem with Jesus' death, it is the hinge on which salvation hangs: 'he was handed over on account of our trespasses and raised on account of our justification'. In Paul's scheme of things that dual happening is that which

61

has altered everything: it explains the past and fulfils it; it has transformed the present; it is the first fruit and assurance of the future consummation. So dominant is it that no other events of Jesus' career play much of a part at all. It is as if, from a 'story' point of view, one is being urged to concentrate at this point, for fear that any distraction would distort the picture. Here is the place to attach faith, first and foremost.

However, no sooner does the matter begin to find expression in written story form than the single-minded clarity begins to evaporate. No longer is the Resurrection at the heart of 'that which yields salvation', playing that part alone, or even supremely. In Mark there is already a two-sided dispersal of attention. On the one side, the episode at the tomb speaks to us of other things, besides the Resurrection of Jesus as salvific. It speaks, for example, of the emptiness of the tomb, which, while it no doubt supports the perception of the Resurrection as saving event, is neither integral nor quite central to it. It also speaks, in a complex and enigmatic way, of testimony to the Resurrection and of its imminent sequel: 'he goes before you into Galilee, there you will see him'. It speaks of silence, speech and fear as somehow involved in discipleship alongside testimony. And it is part and parcel of Mark's pervasive sense of the hardness and mystery of the kingdom of God.

On the other hand, when he sets before us the saving function of Jesus, Mark put it in terms other than that of resurrection, and nowhere does he link it fully and explicitly to the event of Jesus' Resurrection. He puts it, for example, in terms of Jesus' acts of healing and exorcism: it is Jesus' presence, word or act which bring salvation; and in the Gospel as a whole, it is above all his suffering and death which bring it to bear upon us, with overwhelming weight, in the sheer length, detail and theological gravity of the Passion narrative in Chapters 14 and 15. One saying sums up the message: 'the son of man came not to be served but to serve, and to give his life as a ransom for many'. Thus already in the first narrative statement about the rising of Jesus, the Gospel of Mark, the matter is diffused. One could even feel that Mark had deflected attention from it, and critics guess at reasons for such a move: perhaps he faced some such concentration on a triumphalist view of Jesus as that which Paul counteracted earlier at Corinth, and which led him to a similar bringing of attention back to the Cross: 'we preach a crucified Messiah'. Whatever the factors which prompted it, Mark's narrative certainly has the character I have described; and it triggers off a process, it gives a hint which others were not slow to pick up.

By comparison with Mark, Matthew is almost flagrant in his dispersal of conceptual attention to the Resurrection. Non-theological matters step firmly to the fore. Here we have no less than fourteen verses wholly or partly devoted to the purely apologetic question of the guard at the tomb: the assigning of their task, their frightening experience early in the morning, and their being silenced with money at the hands of the high priests and elders. The final episode of the Gospel, the meeting of Jesus with the eleven disciples in Galilee, is in form a Resurrection appearance, but in function it is a great deal wider. It serves as a summary of all Matthew's main themes: Jesus as sovereign, deserving of worship; Christian life as discipleship, learning a skill and an observance; Jesus' role as teacher, leaving to his followers a comprehensive pattern of commands and counsels; and Jesus as present with his own for ever. The angel's appearance is accompanied by the most striking array of phenomena, including even a great earthquake, comparable to the happenings which Matthew describes as taking place at the time of Jesus' death: these events, we are to see, are as important in God's purposes as they could possibly be, bearing all the marks of seers' visions of the coming end of all things. But all this, however striking and however supportive of other beliefs, does little to illuminate faith in the Resurrection itself as God's saving act, true in its own right, the object of single-minded attention.

If we ask the complementary question, where for Matthew the saving effectiveness of Jesus is located, then the answer must lie in his status, as the promised and foretold Messiah,

63

in his life in accordance with that promise and foretelling, and in the teaching he provided for his own.

We have already identified Luke's perspective. Once more, from the point of view of the theological function of Resurrection, there is a blurring of focus, a movement from the centre to the periphery, and a dispersal of interest among a number of new issues. Some of these, like the insistence on Jesus' physicality and on Eucharistic meals of fellowship with him, have all the marks of representing matters of live interest in Luke's day and Luke's circle, just as Matthew's story about the guard surely (and he says as much) related to controversy in his time and setting. And from the point of view of identifying Luke's picture of Jesus' saving role, then the Resurrection is somewhat eclipsed or submerged in a part geographical, part historical process of sacred development which sweeps through Jesus' whole career, onwards and upwards, to heavenly triumph and earthly success in the mission of his followers.

The case of the Gospel of John is different again, and strangely so. It is commonly said that in this Gospel, the ethos of Resurrection pervades the whole, with the episode of the raising of Lazarus playing an explanatory role. There we read that Jesus in his lifetime *is* the Resurrection: if it's Resurrection you're after, it is wherever he is. In so far as this appraisal is correct, then dispersal in one sense has gone very far indeed. But it is only part of the truth. The key move is in the first place verbal. This writer chose to use as his central terms for explicating Jesus' death two verbs most naturally associated with Resurrection: 'exalt' and 'glorify'. Both compel us to see the Crucifixion as the moment of triumph when God's purpose is fulfilled. It is an interpretative move of extreme audacity and power.

There is, however, from the point of view of the centrality of the Resurrection episode itself, a price to pay. If the words and concepts of resurrection are, so to speak, used up in relation to Jesus' person and death, how is the event of Resurrection to be interpreted? What theological work is there left for it to do? Surely, only subordinate functions remain. Like Luke, he tells us that Jesus' risen body was truly physical. By way of Thomas, he tells us of the value of pure faith. By way of meals and meetings, he tells us to depend on Jesus' presence mediated through the Spirit. All are worthwhile points, but none is at the centre of John's theology, and none quite explains to us how the Resurrection event is crucial.

As far as the Gospels, the stories, are concerned, the situation is strange: central as what may be called 'Resurrection faith' undoubtedly was to the early Church, when it comes to content it is as if telling of it made people shy away from it. Story dispersed meaning and pushed it elsewhere.

Evidently, stories are volatile, unstable creatures. They spread, it seems, anyhow, in response to any passing need and interest. Like an easily distracted child, they seem incapable of keeping their attention fixed on a given point. In our sample case, if the datum is taken to be that Jesus' Resurrection is theologically central and in some sense essential to a scheme of salvation, then to let the story be told is to risk that datum's slipping off to play all kinds of unbidden roles. No wonder there were those in early Christianity, like the author of the Pastoral Epistles or 2 Peter, who warned against the entertaining of 'cleverly devised stories' and preferred crisp, succinct, apparently stable statements of faith: they sensed, correctly, where danger lay, if clear and settled doctrine was the requirement. It is, of course, worth reflecting (though this is not the time) in what forms the Resurrection story is now, despite the long fixity of written forms, felt and heard, and what beliefs it now fosters and shelters. As in the Gospels, these beliefs may have the most tenuous logical links with resurrection and be quite capable of standing on their own feet or thriving in other contexts.

The tug between 'story' and 'concept' as vehicles of theological expression, initiated so early, has continued ever since. On the side of 'concept' have stood by far the greater number of the theologians and ecclesiastical authorities, though both have been unwittingly seduced by 'story' more than they have realised. But, like wild flowers growing on the neglected further edges of the garden, 'story' has continued at popular level and among artists and imaginative writers, often frowned upon or brutally suppressed. More important, concepts, doctrines (Resurrection, for instance) never come to us naked, but always interpreted and contextualised.

Nowadays, 'story' is popping up as a category and as a vogue, more or less respectably, all over the place. Within the theological area, it flourishes not only in relation to literature such as the Gospels, where one might expect it, but in relation to subjects such as ethics; and we have books called 'Narrative and Morality', exploring morality in relation to its ever-mobile social and cultural setting. Earlier, I called this approach vague but also helpful and necessary. Philosophical readers will certainly endorse the first adjective; they will perhaps be more reluctant to welcome the others. But vagueness and generality have something to be said for them when it is a matter of exploring a neglected or new mode of perception. As for the necessity: we should note that while we may *become* abstract and clear thinkers, we *are* all (like it or not) the subject of a story of our own, and actors in the stories of others and of the society in which we live. The medium is native to us. And if we are Christian theologians, then behind, in, and among our concepts is inescapably the element of story: both the long, rambling, biblical narrative and the elusive but vivid story of Jesus, inaccessible yet lying close to hand.

To democratise theology and allow narrative its head remains, of course, dangerous. To humanise is to court a certain loss of control. Giving it free rein would, moreover, revolutionise both the character and the agenda of theological discussion. It would, for example, broaden the base in relation to the career of Jesus from which theological reflection and belief may grow: as far back as we can go, we find not hard facts or isolable concepts ('the Resurrection', for example), but the subtlety and mobility of stories. And applied theological tasks, such as some styles of the quest for ecumenical agreement on belief, might come to seem misconceived and even doomed from the start; for the stories of Churches, as of persons, are more volatile, less controllable, than is often supposed. Even a modest injection of the narrative style of theological perception would make development of doctrine easier to understand and to assimilate. It might also contribute to a renewal of that orientation towards the future which was so strong a mark of Christian theology at the beginning: stories and beliefs are always on the move. 'But the word of God is not bound.'

Originally given as an Inaugural Lecture on the author's appointment to a personal chair in Theology, King's College, London, 26 May 1988.

5. Interpreting the Resurrection*

Christopher Rowland

Introduction

Where do we start with an exposition of the New Testament accounts of the Resurrection of Jesus? It is part of conventional wisdom that we must begin with a discussion of the historicity of the account. How far do they correspond to the events in the lives of the first followers of Jesus in the aftermath of his execution? Such an approach seems to be demanded by the treatment of the subject by Paul in 1 Corinthians 15:3ff. He wants to recall the Corinthians to the testimony of those who were Christians before them in order to provide a foundation for their faith. No resolution of the question of the historicity of the Resurrection accounts is going to be possible without attention to philosophical and hermeneutical issues. Are we justified, for example, in reading the Resurrection stories as if they were an exact account of historical events? Wrestling with this is going to be a necessary part of interpreting the New Testament, but that cannot be the end of the story. Even if we conclude that the stories in the Gospels reflect fairly accurately what may have gone on, preoccupation with the historical evidence can never be a substitute for a life lived in obedience to Christ. As the letter of James puts it with regard to faith in God: 'You believe that God is one; you do well. Even the demons believe – and shudder ... faith apart from works is dead' (James 2:19–20). Belief in the Resurrection has never been merely about what may have happened *then*, for it is more

* © Christopher Rowland 1993

about what those who listen to and interpret the story of the Resurrection of Jesus *do* about it themselves. That chimes in with the equal emphasis on the impact of the Resurrection on the disciples in the Gospel accounts. Here commission for service is closely linked with witness to the Risen Christ (see, for example, John 20:21).

A narrow preoccupation with the past can so easily become the be-all and end-all of study of the Resurrection, but this fascination, even obsession, with what actually happened is very much part of the cultural climate of our age. Once we have got to the facts, we feel that we have solved the problem. But that preoccupation can lead us to miss the richness of what the New Testament says about the Resurrection. Passages like Romans 6:4 and Colossians 3:1 can be relegated to mere theologising, the icing on the cake of the quest for the events of the first Easter. That elevation of history above interpretation is something which must be questioned. We are all interpreters whether we are members of the first apostolic group or those who read their testimony. Certainly we are reading and interpreting different signs. Thus we have access to their testimony as well as our own experience of the world, but they too were making sense of their world and the confused signals of their own experience by means of the Bible. *There is no privileged moment when a favoured few saw face to face while the rest of us have to make do with seeing in a glass darkly.* Each generation of interpreters of the Resurrection must explore that subtle interplay of prejudice and experience in the creation of meaning as carefully and critically as possible.

In this essay I therefore want to explore the ways in which we can interpret the Resurrection in the New Testament. I want first of all to ground the New Testament Resurrection accounts in the thought world of Judaism by outlining the background to the Resurrection – doctrine – and by suggesting that a future perspective such as we find in the Book of Revelation encapsulates much of what Resurrection is about. I shall go on to look at the varying concerns of the Gospel narratives before considering the way in which the Resurrection relates to various important New Testament doctrines.

69

I shall conclude by stressing the importance of the Resurrection for maintaining an important critical horizon on Church, theology and politics.

Resurrection: heart of early Christian and Jewish hope

My starting-point for understanding the Resurrection in the New Testament are two passages from Paul (Romans 8 and 1 Corinthians 15) and the Book of Revelation. In all these passages I believe that we find a consistent picture of the Resurrection of Jesus which enables us to see it as a sign of hope for the liberation of humanity and the world and an eschatological horizon which refuses to be entirely Utopian but 'breaks into' the present.[1] In Romans 8 Paul sees the present as a time of tribulation and travail (v. 18), evoking the language of Jewish eschatology and the longing for liberation, but he matches that by stressing the realisation of hope in the activity of the Spirit (v. 23), a present demonstration of the glory to come.

I believe it is impossible to understand the Resurrection in the New Testament without resort to the future hope of Second Temple Judaism.[2] Early Christianity shared with the Pharisees a belief in the resurrection of the dead (Acts 23:6), but regarded this as fulfilled in the case of the Messiah but awaiting completion for the rest of humanity. This is explicit in Paul's writings (for example, Romans 8:21 and 1 Corinthians 15:20), where the future consummation and present fulfilment are linked by the experience of the Spirit as a way of enabling the followers of the Messiah to maintain their assurance that already they were in some sense participating in the glory of the age to come.

A word of caution needs to be entered here. This set of ideas might be loosely referred to as the eschatological contribution of Judaism, but in using that word I am not identifying myself with the belief that some Jews and most early Christians expected the end of the world. Albert Schweitzer put his finger on an important element in Paul's thought when he described the evolution of Paul's mysticism as the modification of Jewish eschatological timetables (though he has helped to muddy the waters of the study of Christian eschatology by his insistence that Jesus and the first Christians expected the end of the world[3]). There is little to suggest that early Christian hopes for the future departed in any significant way from the future hope of groups like the Pharisees. Certainly they wanted to assert that in the case of Jesus an eschatological event had already taken place, but like many other Jews they looked for the realisation of God's kingdom *on earth*.

Evidence of that common heritage may be found in two allusions to contemporary disputes in Mark 12:26ff and Acts 23:6. In the latter passage Paul clearly feels that he is faithfully representing Pharisaic doctrine as against Sadducean. Indeed, according to the Mishnah (Sanhedrin 10:1), belief in the resurrection of the dead had become something of an article of faith for the Pharisaic–rabbinic tradition. The origins of that faith are difficult to determine, as the Old Testament is, by and large, notoriously silent on the subject, the clearest evidence coming from the late book of Daniel (12:2). There are hints to be found elsewhere (for example, Isaiah 26:7 and Hosea 19:25f), but the likehood is that belief in the resurrection of the dead emerged in a situation of political impotence when the ultimate vindication of God's purposes for humanity, particularly for the righteous people, was placed firmly in the future.

At the same time as the beliefs about the resurrection of the dead were emerging, a rather different hope, the immortality of the soul, made its appearance. This is clearly evident in the pre-Christian Wisdom of Solomon, which probably was written in Egypt and thus influenced by the Hellenistic philosophy current in a city like Alexandria. In the past it has been customary to polarise these two forms of eschatological belief as indicative of the material character of Hebrew thought as opposed to the spiritual and dualistic ideas of Greek thought.[4] It is likely, in view of the difficulty of separating Judaism and Hellenism at this period, that they represent rather different preoccupations. Immortality of the soul concentrates on the fate of the individual and promotes a dualistic understanding of the world in which escape from the vicissitudes of existence is a way of release for the righteous. Resurrection of the dead, on the other hand, speaks of the transformation and demonstration of God's righteousness in human history, albeit spoken of in the mythical language appropriate to the dramatic and ultimate activity of God. As such, it refuses to accept that the world will remain as it is and that the poverty of present existence has to be the last word. It may have to be endured, but ultimately those who are 'asleep' will come to see the vindication of the cause of righteousness and the inauguration of God's kingdom.

Revelation: the pattern of promise and fulfilment unveiled[5]

Revelation offers probably one of the most consistent expositions in the New Testament of the cosmic and historical context of divine activity, and as such picks up central themes of the hopes for the future in the prophetic texts of the Old Testament. That view, so deeply embedded in Jewish scripture, was subordinated in due course in mainstream Christian doctrine to concern for the individual soul, a process probably already evident in the New Testament (for example, 2 Corinthians 5:1ff). The struggle between darkness and light in human affairs was neglected in favour of that conflict in the human heart. On the other hand, the Book of Revelation has provided encouragement for all those who look for the fulfilment of God's righteousness in human history. It is no surprise, therefore, that it was this book that was taken as the basis of the historical eschatology of Joachim of Fiore in the thirteenth century, so influential in the millenarian movements in succeeding centuries.[6] It is a book which insistently demands that our theology does not domesticate the Resurrection by depriving it of the power of its historical reference.

The contrast between the vision of the new Jersualem in Chapter 21 and the vision of God in heaven in Chapter 4 should be noted. In Revelation 4 the seer is granted a glimpse of the environs of God. Here God the creator and liberator is acknowledged, and, as we notice from the following chapter, it is from the God of the universe that the historical process begins which leads to the establishment of a new aeon after the manifestation of divine judgement. Redemption and wrath are inextricably intertwined, exactly as in Romans 1:16–17. In the chapters following 4 and 5 we find the picture of a world afflicted but unrepentant, indeed manifesting precisely the kind of misguided devotion to evil which has to be rooted out before God's kingdom can finally come (Revelation 9:20). In Revelation 4 God is still in heaven, and it is there that the heavenly host sing praise and magnify God's name. There is a contrast with Revelation 21 where God's dwelling is on earth; it is no longer in heaven. The division between heaven and earth disappears in the new creation. The tabernacling of God is with humanity; it is then that they will be God's people. God's dwelling is not to be found above the cherubim in heaven; for God's throne is set right in the midst of the New Jerusalem where the living waters stream from the throne, and God's servants, marked with the mark of God, will see God face to face. It is only then that there will be the conditions for God and humanity to dwell in that harmony which was impossible while there was rejection of divine justice. Heaven on earth is what the new age is all about. God is no longer transcendent but immediate – part of that world of perfection and evident in it. Indeed, those who do God's will are God's children, and are identified with the character of God and enjoy God's presence unmediated. In the apocalyptic vision, therefore, the contradictions of a fractured existence are resolved. The whole process climaxing in God tabernacling with humanity had begun with the Lamb's exaltation (Chapter 5). That was a temporary departure from earth, a hidden domination, to be manifested when God would be 'all in all'.

The Resurrection narratives in the canonical Gospels: the story of the Risen Jesus continues in the lives of his followers

At first sight the Gospel narratives seem to exhibit such marked differences. The abrupt ending of Mark's Gospel (whether it was intended or not, we can surely read the text as if it ended at 16:8) contrasts with the rounded endings of Matthew and Luke. The hostility towards Jerusalem in Mark contrasts with the more positive role in salvation history accorded to it in Luke (though by the end of Acts that too must be in doubt). In addition, the lack of Resurrection appearances lend an air of anticipation to the Marcan narrative. This coincides with the muted emphasis on the future glory and the repeated stress on present cost of discipleship throughout the Gospel. It is Mark's Gospel which concludes with outsiders like a centurion, women who had accompanied Jesus and a member of the ruling Council being more concerned with the dying Christ than the male disciples. It is the women who are witnesses of the empty tomb. We are back where we were at the beginning of the Gospel with people on the margins of the world (Mark 1:4), for the Marcan account of the Gospel starts not in Jersualem but with the voice of the prophet in the wilderness. Similarly, it is outside the centre of power that Peter's reconciliation with the Risen Lord must take place, in Galilee.

While the abrupt Marcan ending leaves the reader looking forward to meeting the Risen Jesus in Galilee, away from the city of rebellion, the rounded endings of the other two Synoptic Gospels do not allow the reader to leave the text without being challenged to consider being part of that ongoing history of salvation. The commission in Matthew 28:19 completes the story of Jesus by demonstrating the ineffectiveness of his opponents' attempts to destroy him and offers a note of assurance for those who carry on his work. Their mission is to go out and make all nations disciples and so spread the teaching of Jesus. In Luke the loose ends are tied up by Jesus who shows the close connection between himself and the story of the people of God in the Jewish scriptures. Jesus meets his disciples in the context of meals and as part of the rereading of scriptures in the light of all that had taken place in the experience of those disciples in Jerusalem (Luke 24:18–19).

We should not miss the significance of the ordinariness of the moment as the place of meeting and recognition,[7] something of which Jesus reminds his disciples in the eschatological discourse in Matthew 25:31ff. There the exalted Son of Man turns out in the end to have been the one who meets people in the poor, hungry, naked and imprisoned. The period in Jerusalem in Luke is but a prelude to a continuation of the mission of Jesus to the ends of the earth. The story of the disciples goes on and is left open at the end of Acts with Paul in Rome. They take the place of the Risen Lord. The only closure which Luke–Acts does seem to hint at is the emerging and apparently unbridgeable gap between two rival interpretations of the Jewish tradition, one Messianic, one non-Messianic. Similarly, in John the transfer of Jesus's mission is completed by the sharing of Jesus's charisma: 'As the father has sent me, so I send you. And when he had said this, he breathed on them, and said to them, Receive the Holy Spirit' (John 20:21–22). The disciples are in the upper room for fear of their opponents, temporarily cut off from the world but imminently to join in the witness of the Spirit-Paraclete to the justice of God.[8] The faith in the Risen Jesus in one which does not demand actual tokens: 'Blessed are those who have not seen but yet have believed' (though there is a different emphasis elsewhere in the Johannine tradition which stresses the need for connection with the past – John 19:35 and 1 John 1:1).

Resurrection and the Kingdom of God

Resurrection in the New Testament is to be closely linked with Jesus' proclamation of the reign of God. Jesus proclaimed the imminence of that reign but not its arrival (Luke 11:20) and offered a proleptic glimpse of what it might mean in his acts and words as well as the pattern of life of himself and his circle. Similarly, in proclaiming the Resurrection of Jesus the first Christians regarded this as a sign of the imminence of God's reign and as a demonstration of that which is to come. Thus there is continuity between the mission of Jesus and the proclamation about him. The kerygma of the early Church that Jesus was raised from the dead is another way of expressing that same message of Jesus that the reign of God is at hand; in Jesus' Resurrection the age to come has assuredly drawn near. Thus, Resurrection faith is bound to send us back to the story of Jesus the Messiah and the dawning of the reign of God.

The speeches in Acts (such as Acts 2:23, 3:13ff., 5:30) speak of the Resurrection as the moment when God vindicated Jesus of Nazareth. The material in the Acts speeches can seem a mere reversal by God of the folly and ignorance of human frailty. The wisdom of God is shown to be contrary to human expectations and wisdom; it mirrors the martyrs' vindication in Daniel 12:2 (cf. Wisdom 3–4 and 2 and 4 Maccabees). But there is more to it than that. It is important that this life, with its claim to proclaim the nearness of the fulfilment of God's ultimate purposes, is shown to be true by the demonstration in human history of the reign of God. In these speeches and elsewhere in the New Testament the Resurrection points forward to the moment when what has been only partially accomplished will be completed. Then humanity will realise the ultimate significance of what has already happened in Jesus (Revelation 1:9: 'they shall look upon him whom they pierced'; cf. Mark 14:62). As well as being forward-looking, a Gospel of Resurrection expresses the paradigmatic character of that particular career devoted to God's Kingdom.

A Resurrected Jesus

Early Christians expressed their faith in a *resurrected* Jesus. That must be taken seriously, and we should not assume that this was the way they had to talk about what was going on because the language of resurrection was the only way in which they could express the belief that they had seen Jesus alive. It is unlikely that there was a time within early Christianity when there was a way of speaking about Jesus after his death in ways not affected by resurrection. The statements 'Jesus is alive' or 'I have seen the Lord' (1 Corinthians 9:1) are often taken as indications of another way of expressing the Resurrection faith.[9]

In the New Testament, resurrection and exaltation are themes which are intimately interwoven. Thus it is not easy to separate them one from another and argue for chronological priority. In passages like Philippians 2:6–11, by common consent a very early piece of theological reflection, the theme of exaltation of Christ is stated without explicit reference to the Resurrection. This could appear to give some credence to the idea that, from a very early stage, exaltation was seen as an alternative to Resurrection language. That theory has an air of plausibility when one notes its dominance within the Fourth Gospel and the Letter to the Hebrews, and particularly the uneasy relationship between the theme of exaltation of the Son of Man and the Resurrection narratives in the former. But even in Philippians 2 it is apparent that an eschatological fulfilment is strongly asserted in the use of Isaiah 45 at the climax of the passage. The demonstration of the lordship of Christ reflects the conviction of a radical change in the order of things preparatory to the acknowledgement of God's way. This is exactly what we find in 1 Corinthians 15, where exaltation is seen as part of the much larger eschatological picture in which the consummation of all things involves a vindication and demonstration of the Resurrection of Jesus and recognition of his hitherto hidden sovereignty.

We know that Jesus' first followers had come to discipleship amid the fervour of Messianic expectation. Thus, whatever the effects of the particularities of their experience on their reading of the scriptures, their understanding of Jesus would have been shot through from the very start with Jewish eschatology. Resurrection, therefore, is language which is used deliberately and chosen from a range of options available. Jews of the period were familiar with legends which spoke about significant figures of their past being exalted, either without death as in the case of Enoch (in some versions of the legends, such as in 1 Enoch) and Elijah, or

77

Moses, whose body was never found after death. But Jesus's post-mortem existence was not just an example of an apotheosis; he was the Messiah. The contours of what it was appropriate to say about him needed the language of eschatology to make sense of who he had been. Thus, the way in which Christians talked of the executed Messiah after his death as one whom God had raised from the dead cannot easily be separated from the traditions that the tomb where he had been buried was empty.

A wedge should not be driven between the testimony in 1 Corinthians 15 and the Resurrection narratives in the Gospels. The centrality of resurrection in Paul's thought should give us pause before we attempt to argue for the secondary character of the narratives in the Gospels. The particular choice of discourse used of the fate of the crucified Jesus is related to the eschatological convictions of the earliest disciples. As much as one would like to be able to sidestep the awkward historical questions, the New Testament writings demand that we do not seek refuge from their uncomfortable challenge by resort to present experience of the Resurrected Christ.[10]

If we maintain that the empty tomb traditions are not later legendary accretions, that raises questions to which we long to know the answers such as: What happened to the body of Jesus? While not deterring the quest for answers to that kind of question, it seems to me that the New Testament indicates that our concerns ought to be *primarily* elsewhere. In speaking of the community of those who are his followers as the Body of Christ (1 Corinthians 12; Romans 12), Paul demands that the present dimension of the risen life of Christ in his followers is in part an answer to questions about the presence of the Risen Christ. Similarly, the presence of the Risen Son of Man in the weak and powerless (Matthew 25:31ff) is a cogent reminder that the priorities must not start with speculation about what happened to Jesus but where he may be met *now,* for that is a matter of eternal importance (Matthew 25:45).

Of course, the idea of the exaltation of Jesus in the New Testament offers the possibility of a very different reading of the Resurrection tradition which allows accommodation with the present order. Thus the dualism of heaven and earth resolved in the eschatology of Revelation can be seen as part of the order of things eternally. Salvation then becomes a matter of escape from one realm to the other rather than the resolution of the contradiction between them. Communion with the Risen Jesus can be seen above all as the ability to see behind the veil to where Jesus is exalted in glory (Hebrews 6:19–20) and the goal of discipleship can be seen as glory in the fellowship of the faithful when this earthly pilgrimage is over. Such a view can be gained by a selective reading of New Testament material, but is done at the expense of evacuating the language of Resurrection of its theological power. God has ceased to be God of the universe in travail when it is abandoned to its steady demise as the elect merely have to pursue the way of the heavenly pioneer into the holy place. The ecclesia becomes the outpost of that holy place above whither the souls of the elect are bound for eternity. *Resurrection faith will not permit the abandonment of the hope of the transforming power of God's justice in history.*

The Spirit, Resurrection and eschatology

Whatever views we may have about the part inaugurated eschatology may have played in the messages of Jesus, there can be little doubt that the New Testament writers wanted to stress the present dimension of eschatology. Resurrection had already happened in Jesus' case, and the Spirit was already the pledge of something greater still to come (Romans 8:23; 2 Corinthians 1:22). Most New Testament writers would have accepted the conviction of the writer of the letter to the Hebrews that the followers of Jesus had already tasted of the powers of the age to come in the midst of the old order (Hebrews 6:4–5).

If we take Paul as the dominant witness we can see that this had several consequences. Firstly, a connection was made between the future hope and the story of Jesus. Eschatology became in some sense also Christological, for there was a need for connection with the historical specificity of Jesus' career (1 Corinthians 15 and 1 John 1:1). Secondly, the Resurrection of Jesus was not merely a past story which became part of the Messianic community but demanded of those who responded to that story as good news that they be identified with the Crucified and Risen Jesus as a basis for action in the present (Romans 6:4; cf. Colossians 3:1). Thirdly, Paul's identification of all believers with the Messiah and his mission meant that the life of the Messianic community was seen in *its* historical specificity to be the practical demonstration of the nearness of the reign of God and a challenge to each generation and culture.

Paul's initial conviction may have been to stress a present realisation of hope in all its fullness, though there is little doubt that in the canonical letters this has been tempered by a clear eschatological reservation in which the glorious fulfilment of hope is still awaited. That did not prevent Paul (if it was Paul who wrote Colossians) using the language of fulfilment in Colossians 3:1; and we may suspect that some of those whose views are criticised from time to time in the Pauline corpus for a realised eschatology found much in Paul's preaching and correspondence which seemed to point in that direction (1 Corinthians 4:8 and 2 Timothy 2:18). Enthusiasm, which led to the fantasy that the kingdom of God had already arrived and pretended that the world of oppression and darkness had somehow been completely overcome, was repudiated by Paul in his letters. But that should not blind us to the way in which he speaks of the present. He may be clear that the resurrection of the dead is certainly not already past; but he comes very close at times to overlooking the recalcitrant hostility of the old order. A claim such as that in 1 Corinthians 2:10–13 can easily lead to an overoptimistic practice and a zeal bordering on the fanatical, as may have been the case among some Christians at Corinth.

Resurrection and Parousia

The Pauline treatment of resurrection, as we have seen, leaves us in no doubt that the Resurrection of Jesus is part of a much bigger hope for the future which will only come to completion in the future when the reign of the Messiah and the resurrection of all the dead finally takes place. The links between the Resurrection of Jesus and the eschatological fulfilment became more tenuous, particularly as there was greater concentration on the time between Resurrection and Parousia. The eschatological connotations of both were easily lost. Just as the Resurrection could be used as a metaphor of the new life of the believer in the new age in passages like Colossians 3:1 and the Gnostic Epistle to Rheginos 49:15–16, so also the Parousia of Christ could be linked with the present life of the ecclesia, or the presence of Christ in his apostolic representative and its connection with the climactic moment lost.

The non-appearance of the kingdom presented problems for early Christianity, yet it had ample resources for dealing with it. This may help to explain why we find so little evidence of disappointment with the delay of the kingdom. Apocalyptic writers were convinced that divine glory was not reserved solely for the New Age. The glory which John of Patmos glimpsed in heaven in his Revelation was a matter of living experience here and now for those who confessed Jesus as Messiah and participated in the eschatological spirit. Already those who possessed the spirit of God were sons and daughters of God; already those in Christ were a new creation and a temple of the divine spirit. That hope for the final resolution of the contrast between heaven and earth was already perceived by those who had eyes to see and know it.

An apocalypse like Revelation is interested in the world above, where God's reign is acknowledged by the heavenly host and where the apocalyptic seer can have access to the repository of those purposes of God for the future of the world. Thus the apocalyptic seer can glimpse in the heavenly books the glorious mysteries of past, present and

81

future or be offered a preview of what will happen in human history in the future. That experience of a disclosure of the heavenly mysteries is normally reserved for the apocalyptic seer, but it was perfectly possible to extend that privilege to a wider group. It is that which we find in different forms in some of the Dead Sea Scrolls, such as the Hadayoth (1QH) and later in the Christian hymn book the Odes of Solomon, both of which offer the elect group a present participation in the lot of heaven and a foretaste of the glory which is to come. The identification of the assembly of the elect with Christ in the heavenly places is stressed in the letter to the Ephesians (1:21; cf. 3:5ff), so that the present life of the Church becomes a glimpse, a foretaste of the kingdom of God, just as the Spirit enables the believers to regard the present as a participation 'in the powers of the age to come' (Hebrews 6:5). Similarly, the eschatological vision of the heavenly Son of Man may be glimpsed by those with eyes to see in the persons of the insignificant and lowly (cf. Matthew 25:31ff).

Resurrection: maintaining a critical horizon

As I mentioned in connection with the exaltation traditions in the New Testament, it was quite possible to detach them from the eschatological hope. They could be used as a means of offering hope in another world where Christ is seated at God's right hand in the face of the permanence of a world alien to God. Heaven could then be a haven where the beleagured soul could ascend where Christ had gone before. In the early Church, accommodation with the existing order and a growing concentration on theology and the life of the Church was matched by a diminution of interest in the expectation of a coming reign of the Messiah on earth. Of course, the hope for the reign of God on earth persisted within the early Church,[11] particularly among groups which were marginalised by the emerging dominant ideology.

When Messianic beliefs moved to different settings and into different social strata, the socio-economic reality was bound to have an effect on those ideas. In due course, for example, the title Christ became little more than a proper name and the connections with Jewish Messianism and eschatology were to a large extent lost. The radical political thrust of Messianic beliefs was influenced by shifts in social economic settings and a change in the core meaning of dominant ideas. Then they can be accommodated into a dominant ideology with their cutting edge blunted. The Resurrection tradition was part of a similar development. The way in which the Resurrection material became primarily the belief in personal immortality illustrates the way the Resurrection hope was confined to personal survival and a private religion rather than the central affirmation about the transformation of the universe (such as we find, say, in Romans 8). Preoccupation with the age to come can, of course, be a distraction from the demands of the present. Nevertheless, the language of hope can enable us to maintain a critical reserve towards present arrangements and see the present moment as presenting a challenge to offer a glimpse in our practice of the reign of God which is to come.[12]

We live in an age when the eschatological symbols of the Bible are being put to a variety of uses. There is great interest in the Book of Revelation and related passages. This is not the preserve of the religious right, for liberation exegesis in the basic ecclesial communities of Latin America indicates the centrality of these images for their understanding of their struggle. That tradition rooted in the scripture reminds us that the Resurrection is part and parcel of Christian hope and is itself at the very centre of New Testament faith and practice. A hope for the transformation of society should be at the centre of Christian theology, and it should not be dismissed as a fringe phenomenon. As we seek to explore what role it can play in living the life of Kingdom, the pattern of the Crucified Messiah will contribute to the process of laying bare the various interests at work in the ways in which Resurrection faith has been and is being used. But in the last analysis such hermeneutical activity is ancillary to the meaning of resurrection which is lived, struggled, protested, and reconciled in the midst of death. Unless the Resurrec-

CHRISTOPHER ROWLAND

tion means the transformation of the world in actual practice today it ends up as a tempting ideology which may even blind us to the suffering and injustice of God's world.

Notes

1. This aspect of eschatology is not treated in sufficient depth in P. Carnley, *The Structure of Resurrection Belief* (Oxford: Oxford University Press, 1987), though note the concise introduction to these issues in P. Selby, *Look for the Living* (London: SCM, 1976).
2. On this see G. Nickelsburg, *Resurrection, Immortality and Eternal Life in Intertestamental Judaism* (Cambridge, Mass.: Harvard University Press; London: Oxford University Press, 1972), H. Cavallin *Life after Death* (Lund: Gleenep, 1974), and E.P. Sanders, *Judaism* (London: SCM, 1992).
3. An example of Schweitzer's contribution to this debate may be found in *The Mysticism of Paul the Apostle* (London: A & C Black, 1931); cf. T.F. Glasson, *Jesus and the End of the World* (London, 1980).
4. So O. Cullmann, *Immortality of the Soul or Resurrection from the Dead* (London, 1958).
5. This is a summary of material in C. Rowland, *Radical Christianity* (Cambridge: Cambridge Univeristy Press, 1988), pp. 72ff.
6. See M. Reeves, *Joachim of Fiore and the Prophetic Future* (London: SPCK, 1976) and N. Cohn, *The Pursuit of the Millennium* (London: Secker & Warburg, 1957).
7. See further, N. Lash, *Easter in Ordinary* (London: SCM, 1988).
8. J. Ashton, *Understanding the Fourth Gospel* (Oxford: Oxford University Press, 1992).
9. See, for example, W. Marxen, *The Resurrection of Jesus of Nazareth* (London: SCM, 1970).
10. See C. Rowland, *Christian Origins* (London: SPCK, 1985), pp. 187ff.
11. See B. Daley, *The Hope of the Early Church* (Cambridge: Cambridge University Press, 1991).
12. A good example of the importance attached to resurrection and hope in modern theology may be found in the work of Jürgen Moltmann; see the Introduction by R. Bauckham in Moltmann, *Messianic Theology in the Making* (Basingstoke: Macmillan, 1987).

6. Is the Resurrection a 'Historical' Event? Some Muddles and Mysteries*

Sarah Coakley

Is the Resurrection a 'historical' event? The question is as legitimate, and indeed pressing, as when Paul first posed it thus: 'If Christ has not been raised, then our preaching is in vain and your faith is in vain' (1 Corinthians 15:14). Yet modern theology has, in the main, been notoriously coy about dubbing the Resurrection an event in 'history'. Superficially, this might look like a mere semantic problem, an understandable resistance to describing as 'historical' an event which purportedly transcends the normal course of history. But in fact there have been two more fundamental reasons, as I see it, for resisting an investigation of the Resurrection with the critical tools of the secular historian. The first is theological, the other more strictly philosophical or 'scientific'.

Theologians of the influential 'dialectical' or 'existentialist' camps, first, urged the total inappropriateness of attempting to demonstrate Jesus' divine status out of the materials of secular historical procedure; such, they believed, could only display a kind of 'works righteousness', a futile attempt to encapsulate the divine or eschatological in the web of human categories.[1] To the sceptic, however, such a theological manoeuvre might smack of a certain post-Enlightenment defensiveness: was it after all an attempt to sidestep a second, and more profound *aporia* about the historical investigation of Jesus' post-mortem body? This

* © Sarah Coakley 1993

latter, and second, problem is the difficulty of clarifying the conditions under which a 'miracle' such as the Resurrection could be legitimately and reliably established to have occurred at all. This involves debate about purported violations of 'natural law' in the scientific realm, as well as discussion of the appropriate canons of assessment of historical evidence. Since Hume's classic essay 'Of Miracles' in *An Enquiry Concerning Human Understanding* (1748), this cluster of issues has been debated with ever-increasing sophistication by philosophers of science and religion; and if some theologians have attempted to avoid the complexity of these issues altogether, it may well have been because they sensed that the sceptical or 'positivist' challenge remained formidable. Many would still concur with Hume's much-quoted conclusions that 'the knavery and folly of men are such common phenomena, that I should rather believe the most extraordinary events to arise from their occurrence, than admit of . . . a violation of the laws of nature!'[2]

Thus the theologian who tackles the question of the Resurrection's 'historicity' head-on, and claims that it can be substantiated, is a bold one; and undeniably the most sophisticated attempt to do this in post-war theology remains Wolfhart Pannenberg's early book on Christology, *Jesus – God and Man.*[3] The fascination this volume has exercised on its English readership since its translation in 1968 is not hard to explain: the undeniable finesse of Pannenberg's handling of the evidence about the Resurrection, combined with his Pauline insistence that 'In the Resurrection of Jesus we . . . have to do with the sustaining foundation of the Christian faith',[4] has been greeted with enthusiasm by the conservatively-minded in general.[5] But more specifically, the long-standing tradition in Anglican circles of linking a doggedly *historical* approach to Jesus on the one hand, with a Chalcedonian orthodoxy on the other, finds in Pannenberg a natural, and ready, support. For in virtue of his resurrection argument, Pannenberg paves the way to legitimating Jesus' claim to divine status as 'Son of God', second person of the Trinity.

Pannenberg's argument for the Resurrection's 'historicity'

has come under critical scrutiny from various directions.[6] His own theology, too, has broadened and complexified since *Jesus – God and Man*; and although he has never repudiated what he wrote there, the appearance of his *Systematic Theology* is a timely moment to enquire whether there has been any shift in the approach to the Resurrection that characterised his early work.[7] But it is not the task of this essay to give a full account of the development of Pannenberg's thought, nor to evaluate the range of critical responses to him.[8] Rather, by taking Pannenberg's early work *Jesus – God and Man* as my focus and test case, I hope to illuminate the points in this vexed debate about the Resurrection and 'history' at which 'muddles' obtrude and 'mysteries' impinge.

Some contrapuntal allusions to British analytic philosophy of religion's discussion of 'miracles' will be instructive here, and will help to show how Pannenberg's case could be both clarified and criticised. There are, in fact, striking parallels (somewhat surprising, given the different cultural and philosophical milieus) between Pannenberg's work and that of the British philosopher of religion, Richard Swinburne.[9] But it is perhaps not insignificant that both Pannenberg's *Jesus – God and Man* and Swinburne's early book in defence of miracles, *The Concept of Miracle*, were forged against the backdrop of prevailing philosophical scepticism and positivism of the late 1960s. Both were then courageously defiant in response to it; but neither author would now, I believe, attempt to convince someone of Christian theism in virtue of the evidence for one purportedly miraculous event *alone*. We shall see why this is so by the end of the essay, and thus why Pannenberg's earlier claim is unwise, that 'If this [*sc.* argument for the Resurrection of Jesus] collapses, so does *everything else* which the Christian faith acknowledges.'[10]

It may be helpful to anticipate the structure of my argument in advance of the detailed analysis of Pannenberg's case. It will be clear that I take it as read that it is at least *apologetically* crucial to clarify whether, and how, Christians may appropriately term the Resurrection 'historical'. From here I shall present three theses.

87

First, I shall argue, with Pannenberg (though with a significant modification of his assumptions), that *in principle* the Resurrection may be investigated as a 'historical' event that happened to Jesus' body, and that Christians have a responsibility to pursue this issue critically, and to clarify it.

But second, *in practice*, I shall argue, against Pannenberg, that the available evidence for Jesus' bodily Resurrection is such that the historical route he proposes ends only in unsatisfactorily uncertain conclusions, which cannot hope *per se* to convince the sceptic.

Thirdly, however, I shall propose that in any case, as Pannenberg seems to allow on occasion, an approach to the Resurrection that restricts itself only to a dispassionate 'historical' assessment of evidence for a transformed body of Jesus may prove religiously stultifying. It cannot do justice to the diversity and *richesse*, nor to the appropriate dimension of mystery, which Christian 'Resurrection' language in the broader sense enshrines, and to which the New Testament and tradition witness.

These three conclusions to which I am working will be correlated with the three sections of my exposition of Pannenberg. In the first section I look at the preparatory methodological question of historical analogy; in the second at Pannenberg's handling of the evidence itself; and in the third at his assertions about the meaning of the Resurrection.

The question of historical analogy

Pannenberg has rightly pointed out that debates about the evidence for Jesus' Resurrection are often confused from the start by latent disagreements over the question of historical analogy. As Pannenberg puts it, 'If the historian approaches his work with the conviction that "the dead do not rise", then it has already been decided that Jesus also has not risen'.[11] It is usual to discuss this issue as a straightforward contest between a 'positivist' stance (the view Pannenberg is attacking) and an 'idealist' one: are there any (purported) events which the historian may justifiably rule out *a priori* as impossible, as the positivist claims? In order to adjudicate on this (and here I want to go somewhat beyond Pannenberg), one needs to be careful that the terms in the debate on analogy are clear, for two areas of possible confusion immediately arise here. To begin with, there might be any one of three different types of 'unusual event' in the mind of the disputants; thus the *content* of what is debated needs to be clarified. Secondly, there are two different available understandings of the term 'analogical argument', and so too the *method* in question needs definition. These difficulties overlap, and we shall need to discuss them together.

Let us start by asking in what senses the Resurrection might be described as an 'unusual' or 'unique' event. An 'unusual event' in the strongest sense, first, could be claimed to be one without *any* method appropriate to describe it. Being utterly without parallels it would also be incomprehensible, unintelligible. As we shall see later, there is not a small strand of this sort of talk in Pannenberg himself, though one senses it causes him some embarrassment. For the moment, we must simply note the oddity of appeals to such 'events' as 'historical'; for presumably without *any* means of describing what is supposed to have 'happened', there are equally no means of deciding whether 'it' has or not.

A second way of defining an 'unusual event', at the other end of the scale, would be in terms of something unparalleled in our present time or culture and yet well attested as having happened in the past (while yet not actually involving the violation of natural laws). That rider is important, as we shall see shortly. In the category of 'unusual event' under discussion here all that is required of the historian is a certain leap, or stretching of the imagination. To cite an example provided by R. G. Collingwood:

> That the Greeks and Romans exposed their new-born children in order to control the numbers of their population is no less true for being unlike anything that happens in the experience of contributors to the *Cambridge Ancient History*.[12]

In cases such as these, then, the assimilation by the historian of what is alien to him involves an 'analogical' move from the known to the unknown: the known, in the case of Collingwood's example, being such considerations as the frailty of new-born babies' health, their sensibility to cold, the instances of fatality in cases where a deranged mother has abandoned her child, and so on. The unknown, or 'unusual', factor is the regular occurrence of such events as a socially acceptable practice. This example, then, opens up one understanding of what is meant by 'analogical' argument in the historian's sphere, and it is important to notice that it is only thus that Pannenberg is prepared to admit the usefulness of an analogical method. Analogical argument on this view does not delimit historical possibilities but extends them. Thus 'A genuine extension of knowledge takes place in this way.'[13]

However, we have not yet got to the nub of the problem; for it becomes clear on inspection that the Resurrection as portrayed in the New Testament text falls into neither of the two categories of 'unusual events' so far outlined. Yet a third sense of 'unsual event' is at stake. It is different from the first definition in that it is at least capable of expression in words, even if a satisfactory scientific *explanation* is not immediately obvious. Even so, by the process of analogical movement just described one may conjure up in one's imagination the picture of a man who has died yet returns, whose side may be touched yet who passes through doors like a phantom, who takes breakfast with his followers yet vanishes from sight at will, and who finally disappears upwards into the clouds leaving no trace of himself. On the other hand, the case of the Resurrection, and indeed many other so-called 'miraculous' events, is decisively different from Collingwood's example of infant exposure in that it involves the violation of presently accepted scientific laws (which are assumed, until shown otherwise, to represent regularities of nature itself); notably here the laws of conservation of mass energy and of gravity are flouted, not to speak of the continually reaffirmed biological observation that human bodies do not come alive again some days after death has occurred.

90

It is here, in the face of violated natural laws, that a second type of analogical argument is often invoked, associated with the 'positivist' camp of historians, and this time one that operates negatively. It is this type of argument that Pannenberg deplores.[14] It is the dogmatic banning from historical possibility of anything that contravenes currently accepted laws of science. As expressed classically by F. H. Bradley:

> ... critical history must have a presupposition, and ... this presupposition is the uniformity of law ... history rests in the last resort upon an inference from our experience, a judgment based upon our own present state of things, upon the world personal in us; and ... this is the sole means and justification which we possess for holding and regarding supposed evidence as real, i.e. as members in and of our universe.[15]

At this point an impasse is reached: which sort of analogical argument is appropriate to a decision on the historicity of an 'unusual event' of our third type, that is, the supposed violation of natural law in the past? How is one to adjudicate between the 'idealists' ' desire to apply the first, 'stretched' kind of analogical argument (Pannenberg's position), and the 'positivists' ' insistence on the second? It is important to note that both sides have a tendency to blur the argument by confusing this third type of 'unusual event' with one of the other two that I have distinguished. Thus a possible positivist ploy is to suggest that the violation of natural law creates a picture of such confusion or incoherence that one cannot even say what one *means* has happened; and therefore, the argument continues, there can be no knowing what would constitute the appropriate criteria for assessing the truthfulness of a report, for instance, of a body that is physical enough to be touched, yet non-physical enough to pass through closed doors.[16] Here my third sense of unusual event blurs into the first. However, the exponents of the other use of analogical argument, among them Pannenberg, tend to collapse the distinction between 'unusual events' that do violate a natural law and those that do not, that is, the important distinction between the second and third senses of 'unusual event' that I have outlined. This indeed is my principal criticism of Pannenberg in this section. For his insistence that history is concerned not with universals or laws, but with particulars, seemingly implies that for him the historian's approach to apparent violations of law need not be tempered by any special degree of caution:

> Provided that historical science is occupied above all with the *particularity* and *uniqueness* of phenomena, its interest must therefore be focused more upon the *ever peculiar, non-homogeneous* features, rather than the common ones first obtruded by analogies.[17]

In addition to this blurring of distinctions that both positivists and idealists tend to resort to, I would suggest that both camps have also each overlooked one significant point, and the uncovering of these factors could at least help them to a position of common ground. The significant point overlooked by the positivist side, which Pannenberg himself rightly highlights, is that scientific laws are themselves the products of assessed *evidence*; our present laws are not therefore immutable; and indeed in the past scientists have often made radical changes to laws previously regarded as 'inviolable', and even rejected them completely in favour of new models. Further, the significance of evidence in scientific work opens up a legitimate procedure for evaluating the reports of the (presumed) violation of a law. A glance at this procedure will at the same time reveal the crucial point overlooked by the idealist historians, including Pannenberg.

This is where Swinburne's proficient discussion in *The Concept of Miracle*[18] remains illuminating, both in the areas of scientific procedure and of evaluation of evidence. If a violation of a law is reported, he argues, the scientist has to deal first with the historical problem of the reliability of the testimony involved. This involves a delicate weighing of considerations, but there are appropriate canons of judgement available for the assessment. As David Hume argued in his essay 'Of Miracles', we should *suspect* witnesses' testimony if the witnesses contradict each other, if there are only a few of them, if the witnesses are 'of doubtful character', if they deliver their testimony either with hesitation or with 'too violent asseveration', and particularly if they have an interest in establishing a violation of law (for religious purposes, for instance).[19] But it is not at least *in principle* impossible that a scientist should be confronted with testimony that has every appearance of being reliable and accurate, despite the fact that it implies a violation of a law: it may, in short, be coherent, straightforwardly and calmly attested by a large number of intelligent and honest people, and so on.[20] If this happens, the scientist should, first, consider the possibility of modifying the original law L to make a new law L^1 which will effectively account for the 'violation' and be capable of predicting similar occurrences.[21] But there is a sliding scale here: a modification might make the new law L^1 so cumbersome or contradictory that it would be less effective than the original L in its capacity to predict and explain. If this is the case, the instance simply has to be described as a real 'violation'; the law remains a law, but it is now allowed a 'non-repeatable' exception.[22]

This granted, if we return now to the debate between the two historians' schools: as we have seen, the *positivists* need to be reminded that they may not legitimately rule out a violation of law *a priori* but instead use appropriate canons of judgement to evaluate the available evidence. One could say that they are chided by the Humean dictum, 'The wise man . . . proportions his belief to the evidence.'[23] The *idealists*, however, among them Pannenberg, have overlooked the significance of another of Hume's conclusions, that 'no testimony is sufficient to establish a miracle [understood as a violation of a law] unless the testimony be of such a kind that its falsehood would be more miraculous than the fact which it endeavours to establish.'[24] In other words, and this is the important point in concluding this section, the burden of proof lies very squarely, in the discussion with the *secular* historian or scientist, with the one claiming that a violation has taken place. It is this, as we shall show further below, that Pannenberg is not willing to admit in *Jesus – God and Man*, and we shall go on to explain how it ill affects his argument on the Resurrection. Swinburne, in contrast, does admit the point; and so he has to resort, in *The Concept of Miracle*, to some drastically unrealistic examples of the 'miraculous' in order to clarify the conditions under which even the secular observer would be obliged to admit that a divine intervention had occurred. (Significantly, he does not attempt to tackle the delicate question of the Resurrection here.)[25] We shall return later to the issue of the extent to which both authors may have now modified their attempt to meet the sceptic head-on on the issue of 'miracle' alone; but for the meantime we shall pursue our investigation on *Jesus – God and Man* and turn to Pannenberg's handling of the evidence for the Resurrection itself.

The historical evidence

We have already noted that several 'natural' laws are violated in the New Testament narratives of the Resurrection, and we now see that, though such violations cannot be ruled out *a priori*, testimony of a very reliable variety is required in order for one to judge such occurrences as successfully corroborated. One realises immediately, however, and this without needing to delve into a proliferation of detail, that a series of problematic features about the New Testament account at once appear to render such a hopeful outcome unlikely. These features can be stated succinctly:

1. None of the Gospels describes the event of the Resurrection itself. Instead they tell of the consequences of it: the appearance of Jesus in pseudo-physical form. So there is no evidence concerning the transformative process through which his dead body supposedly went.

2. The accounts fall into two categories (the 'appearance' and 'grave' traditions, respectively) which exhibit divergent features. For instance, Paul's account in 1 Corinthians 15 talks of the appearances without speaking of Jesus' corporeal features; indeed the implications are that such features are largely irrelevant (v. 50). And there is no discussion of the empty tomb, despite the note that Jesus was indeed buried (v. 4). All this stands in a problematic relationship to the stories in the Synoptics and John.

3. In turn, the empty tomb or 'grave' traditions themselves

contain numerous contradictions concerning the people who went to the tomb, what or whom they found there, and the places where subsequent appearances occurred (Mark 16 and parallels).

4. They also exhibit all the signs of an accumulating tradition, with increasing interest in the manifestly supernatural (e.g. Matthew 27:51f and 28:2f), in the corporeal features of the risen body (Luke 24:41–3, John 20:27) and in apparently apologetic motifs, such as Matthew's story of the guard on the tomb (Matthew 27:64f) or the bribing of the soldiers to say that the body was stolen (Matthew 28:12f).

5. The only testimony we have is from Christian sources, where an interest is clearly at stake.

Enough has already been said to show that this testimony falls under several of Hume's bans, mentioned earlier, concerning the possible unreliability of eyewitness reports. Thus any attempt to establish the historicity of the Resurrection has a more than unusually heavy 'burden of proof' on its shoulders if it is to convince the sceptic, a burden arising not only from the issue of 'law violation' but also exacerbated by the nature of the available evidence. With this in mind, we turn to Pannenberg's own evaluation of this evidence in *Jesus – God and Man.*

The first point to notice is that he takes the separateness of the two strands of tradition – the 'appearance' and the 'grave' strands – as a factor that could have *positive* implications. If the appearance and grave traditions could be shown to have come into existence independently, this would be a point in favour of the Resurrection's historicity, he says.[26] Accordingly, he examines these two traditions separately, and in both cases his argument is undergirded by a number of assumptions. We need to excavate and analyse these assumptions in order to evaluate the argument as a whole. Treating the first of the appearances, the following assertions become explicit from Pannenberg.

1. Pannenberg insists that Paul's first encounter with the Risen Christ was qualitatively different from later revelations (such as the experience described in 2 Corinthians 12), and

that generally 'primitive Christianity itself apparently knew how to distinguish between ecstatic visionary experience and the fundamental encounters with the risen Lord.'[27]

To this, however, one may reply that for Paul the Damascus road encounter would have been 'fundamental' and 'different' primarily in the sense that it was his *first* revelation and his conversion experience; that it is quite possible that the 'appearance' to the five hundred in 1 Corinthians 15:6 (which for Pannenberg has to count as a fundamental 'Resurrection' appearance) refers to his experience at Pentecost – which at least according to Acts did not involve a revelation of Jesus personally (Acts 2:1f) and further that, as Pannenberg himself admits, interestingly, the experience on the Damascus road displays all the characteristics of a 'visionary' occurrence.[28] In short, any supposed categorising of appearances could not in itself sway one towards regarding *Paul's* first revelation as having some 'extra-subjective reality' which the other did not.[29]

2. Pannenberg's second assumption emerges thus: 'The Easter appearances are not to be explained from the Easter faith of the disciples; rather, conversely, the Easter faith of the disciples is to be explained from appearances.'[30]

This is undoubtedly a strong point, but Pannenberg's insistence that 'Something like this did not arise as the *mental reaction* to Jesus' catastrophe'[31] is not in itself – as he assumes – an argument against a 'subjective-vision hypothesis'. It would certainly, I think, be difficult to account for the appearances as the result of a conscious mental deduction on the disciples' part; but 'reactions' can also be subconscious and surprising; I think there is no doubt that the disciples did undergo some unexpected experiences without which one could not account for their faith in a Risen Christ. But again, this is no demonstration *in itself* of an 'extra-subjective reality' being involved.

3. Pannenberg further appeals to 'the number of the appearances and their temporal distribution'.[32] However, while one certainly should always be wary of rejecting a large amount of *coincident* evidence, when the evidence is at many points contradictory and when the individual parts of it do

not convince one of a law violation, then clearly the argument is hardly strengthened by the multiplication of instances.

4. Most significantly, Pannenberg's attempt to rule out 'vision' as a suitable category for explanation most revealingly indicates his assumption about the burden of proof:

> The psychiatric concept of vision, *which is primarily derived from the investigation of mentally ill persons*, cannot be applied without further ado to phenomena in the history of religions. If by 'vision' one understands a psychological event that is without a corresponding extra-subjective reality, then one can certainly not presuppose such a 'subjective' concept of vision for the resurrection appearances as self-evident. Only if the corresponding psychiatric point of contrast can be inferred from the texts could this understanding of vision be used.[33]

Here, Pannenberg appears to be insisting that it is up to the sceptic to demonstrate that the disciples were 'ill' before doubts should be cast on the issue of an extra-subjective reality. But surely the point (that we have already laboured) is that it lies primarily with Pannenberg to give convincing evidential arguments for the presence of an extra-subjective being, not with his opponents to prove its absence, as he seems to suppose. In addition, this argument involves Pannenberg in the questionable assumption that only 'madmen' have visions, which, incidentally, should embarrass him, because he is quite willing to admit that Paul had visions (as in 2 Corinthians 12), and presumably he is not wishing to imply that Paul was mentally ill.

Turning to the 'grave' tradition, I would suggest that we find a couple of similarly dubious assumptions from Pannenberg.

1. There is a particular stress on a rigorous fact-proving contest which Pannenberg supposes would immediately have sprung up in Jerusalem between the disciples and the Jews: 'the proclamation of the news of Jesus' resurrection in Jerusalem, which had established the Christian community, is hardly understandable except under the assumption that Jesus' tomb was empty.'[34] And this is because: 'How could

97

Jesus' disciples in Jerusalem have proclaimed his resurrection if they could be constantly refuted merely by viewing the grave in which his body was interred?'[35]

Now this last part is certainly an important question; but we have to ask: what evidence Pannenberg is drawing on here? To begin with, it seems that the empty-tomb stories may not have circulated very early. But further, are we certain that the *disciples* knew where Jesus was buried? Oddly enough, Pannenberg himself seems to waver on this point, at one moment rejecting as 'practically irrelevant' the suggestion that the disciples were ignorant of the whereabouts of Jesus' tomb,[36] and at the next admitting that 'According to the oldest strata of the tradition, the disciples did not show any concern for the empty tomb.'[37] However, his reconstruction seems to rest on another assumption.

2. If the Jews had been unconvinced by the Christian claims, says Pannenberg, they would certainly have recorded their objections and rebuttals, and the fact that we have no early independent Jewish remarks of this sort is thus probably a sign that the tomb was empty. Further:

> Among the general historical arguments that speak for the trustworthiness of the report . . . is, above all, the fact that the early Jewish polemic against the Christian message about Jesus' resurrection, traces of which have already been left in the Gospels, does not offer any suggestion that Jesus' grave had remained untouched. However, quite to the contrary, it shared the conviction with its Christian opponents that Jesus' grave was empty.[38]

Pannenberg presumably means the story in Matthew 28:13 when he talks of 'traces' of early Jewish polemic. But have we any reason to believe that this apologetic elaboration ('His disciples came by night and stole him away while we were asleep') was actually the rejoinder from Jewish opponents in the earliest days in Jerusalem, and this because they themselves realised that the tomb was empty? Without any support from Jewish documents that can soundly be established as contemporary, Pannenberg's argument turns out to have no firm basis; it is indeed a classic instance of an argument from silence.

We have now looked in detail at the various assumptions which undergird Pannenberg's treatment of the two separate strands of evidence for the Resurrection. He concludes his review of these two strands with this remark:

> If the appearance tradition and the grave tradition came into existence independently, then by their mutually complementing each other they let the assertion of the reality of Jesus' resurrection ... appear as historically very probable, and that always means in historical inquiry that it is to be presupposed until contrary evidence appears.[39]

Now enough has already been said to show that neither of the two strands has the independent strength that Pannenberg intends, and without this veracity of their own it is doubtful whether their separate growths could help to strengthen the case against the 'subjective' vision hypothesis. Rather, the points of *divergence* between the two strands make one all the more wary of the quality of the evidence. This particular failure of Pannenberg to counter the problems attached to the New Testament evidence is not the only one, however. The problem of religious *interest*, as we have noted, is undeniable; and the other difficulties intrinsic to the material that we noted at the beginning of this section will be taken up again as we now gather the results of this part of the essay.

First, we have seen that as far as the 'grave' tradition is concerned, Pannenberg's attempt to demonstrate that Christians and Jews alike knew the whereabouts of Jesus' tomb, and also that it was empty, rests on frail assumptions. But further, he does not seem much interested in countering the difficulties either of the divergent evidence or of the accumulation of legendary tradition. In fact he admits at the beginning of his presentation in *Jesus – God and Man* that one cannot use the Gospels as sources of information about the details of the *appearances* because:

> The appearances reported in the Gospels, which are not reported by Paul, have such a strong legendary character that one can scarcely find a historical kernel of their own in them. Even the

99

Gospels' reports that correspond to Paul's statements are heavily coloured by legendary elements, particularly by the tendency toward underlining the corporeality of the appearances.[40]

With this admitted, but with Pannenberg's own conclusions about the tomb strongly questioned, one can only say, with critical honesty, that the 'grave' traditions provide insufficient evidence to establish any conclusion with strong certainty. And yet there remains something irreducible about them from the historical angle that makes it impossible to discount them *in toto* as fabrications of the early Church. As has been well pointed out: 'If the empty tomb story had really been created subsequently to convince doubters, the Church could surely have made a better job of it. It rested entirely on the testimony of women (which in Jewish law was not binding) . . .'[41] In short, the 'grave' narratives seen to have *some* historical germ, but the fragmentary evidence leaves us with little more than an elusive, beckoning question mark.

Turning secondly to the 'appearance' traditions, one can say with more certainty that it was these revelations to the Apostles (1 Corinthians 15) that were crucial for the founding of the Church. But the main point in hand is Pannenberg's attempt to establish unequivocally the 'extra-subjective reality' of Jesus in the appearances, and this, as I hope I have shown, lacks good evidential support. Moreover, the strength of his conclusions rests on a fundamental misapprehension about the burden of proof, which is all the more obvious in his final remark quoted above: the reality of Jesus' Resurrection is 'historically very probable, and that always means . . . it is to be presupposed until contrary evidence appears.' This is, of course, the correct procedure in normal circumstances, but we need here to drive home the results gained from our earlier discussion on analogy. We are dealing in this case with purported violations of natural law; and that means that scepticism is appropriate until substantial evidence in favour of the violation is provided. Curiously, Pannenberg can at times come close to admitting this;[42] but it is not the dominant tone of his discussion in *Jesus – God and*

Man, and nor can it be, granted the systematic centrality that he accords there to the success of his historical argument.

By now, only the first problematic quality of the evidence that we mentioned earlier – the obvious fact that there is no description of the Resurrection itself – has not been re-examined. But the significance of this difficulty rapidly becomes apparent in Pannenberg's argument. For one needs to remember that the implication of this gap in our evidence is that all the New Testament narratives are themselves in some sense already interpretations. More important, they are interpretations from a first-century Jewish perspective. The part that an alien world-view plays in Pannenberg's construction, and, more generally, the sort of *significance* that historians consider appropriate to ascribe to the events with which they deal, is the question to which we must now turn. Here we shall see again that our own conclusion so far – that the 'historical' investigation of the Resurrection ends in unsatisfactory enigma – is far from acceptable to Pannenberg, indeed is duly turned on its head.

The meaning of the Resurrection

The controversial argument that Pannenberg adduces at this point in *Jesus – God and Man* is that only an interpretation from the perspective of first century apocalyptic will do for this event. There are, it seems, two prongs to this argument, which I shall treat separately.

The first runs as follows:[43] the evidence concerning the Resurrection is not explicable in terms of *known* laws of nature: we therefore have no adequate categories at our disposal with which to describe what happened and so must resort to the categories used at the time:

> If the resurrection or the appearances of the resurrected Jesus were only brute facts without inherent significance, then, certainly, the origin of faith would not be understandable from this event. But that event had its own meaning within its sphere in the history of traditions: the beginning of the end, the confirmation and exaltation of Jesus by God himself, the ultimate

demonstration of the divinity of Israel's God as the one God of all men.[44]

It turns out, then, that not only are we to deduce the violation of several natural laws from the fragile evidence we have, but also some very weighty theological judgements. One should note, however, in this talk of 'inherent significance' that Pannenberg is not asserting baldly that *all* past events should be granted by historians the significance attached to them originally. For one thing, he explicitly rejects the possibility of a direct psychological empathy with the past, which might have helped him to argue such a point. Commenting on Wilhelm Dilthey's 'idealistic' doctrines of *Nacherleben* and *Verstehen* (the 'reliving' and 'understanding' of past actions), he argues:

> It is really extremely questionable that any average historian *by virtue of his having the same psychic nature,* can 'empathize' with any activity of men of earlier time he pleases, whether they be criminals, founders of religion, or rulers.[45]

Further, Pannenberg is strongly aware of the importance of the historian's critical autonomy in every generation. This is already clear from his treatment of the New Testament evidence, where it is obviously his desire to work through the arguments again for himself. He says elsewhere that:

> In spite of our statement that the meaning of an event is inherent to its original context and is not something injected into it by the interpreter, nevertheless that meaning can be determined only in relation to the vantage point of the particular inquirer.[46]

Pannenberg's hermeneutic is a sophisticated one, based largely on the work of H.-G. Gadamer; it involves the assumption that the hermeneutical task has to be constantly revised within an expanding context of meaning which will only be available in its totality at the end of time. Each revision is in its own way an 'anticipation' of that full meaning to be revealed at the *eschaton*.[47] Hence it is only in this one case of the Resurrection, it seems, that we are bound by the original apocalyptic categories of interpretation, and this, it is claimed, is because we have no other way to deal with this unique event.

This is a highly significant move in Pannenberg's argument, but a questionable one for at least two reasons:

1. The results gleaned from the discussion of the historical evidence have already made it clear that there are other categories available for interpreting the evidence, not least the 'vision' hypothesis; and intra-Christian interpretations of the Resurrection, too, have been many and various, and far from restricted to the original first-century Palestinian ones.

2. Again, and more significantly, Pannenberg's argument here contains a latent circularity. For the disciples an apocalyptic conception of history was natural, and it was thus in those categories that they interpreted their experiences. Conversely, if we, as products of twentieth-century culture, could be convinced of the historicity of the Resurrection of Jesus we might wish to reinstate a theory of *general* resurrection. But what is not legitimate, surely, is Pannenberg's move *in our case* from general resurrection to Jesus' Resurrection. For we should need to be already agreed on the usefulness of the apocalyptic language of a general resurrection before the argument could have any force.

However, it is here that Pannenberg introduces his second argument in favour of adopting an apocalyptic interpretation of the Resurrection. In fact he even admits the weakness of the first when he says:

> The expectation of resurrection must be presupposed as a truth that is given by tradition or anthropologically or is established philosophically when one speaks about Jesus' resurrection.[48]

This is an important admission. Pannenberg actually chooses the 'anthropological' route in *Jesus – God and Man*: it belongs to the essence of humanity, the argument goes, to find no 'ultimate fulfilment' in the finitude of earthly life, and thus it is natural to hope beyond death.[49] And this hope, which all share, consciously or unconsciously, is most adequately expressed in terms of resurrection from the dead.

Again, however, there seem to be potential flaws in this argument:

1. First, there is a certain imperialism in Pannenberg's insistence that hope beyond death is fundamental to human nature, especially when he himself admits that 'modern man apparently lives surprisingly well without being disturbed by the question about death'.[50] This picture Pannenberg of course rules out as 'deceptive'; but one could certainly make a good case against him in this regard. Indeed, could one not claim that our so-called 'materialist' society exhibits those very features described by Pannenberg as indicating a *lack* of concern about life after death? For he admits again:

> Only if this individual man ... is ... completely absorbed in humanity as it is at hand in his concrete society, only then would the idea of a life beyond death be something to be relinquished.[51]

2. Secondly, the way Pannenberg has to equate concern with life after death solely with the Jewish apocalyptic view of the Resurrection appears even more suspect. To do so he first has to presume that first-century Palestinian Judaism was itself at base united in its belief in 'a *general* resurrection; and this is a complex and contentious matter, as Pannenberg is well aware.[52] To go on with, he then has to demythologise the idea of resurrection from the dead so that it is well-nigh unrecognisable. (To give one 'secularised' version of his: 'This metaphor indicates that the destination of individuals is not exhausted in the service of a social order that has become autonomous in relation to them.'[53]) But then he has to rule out other possible candidates by further appeals to modern anthropology. ('What was once distinguished as body and soul is considered today as another mode of the *whole* man.'[54]) Even if this argument were taken as sufficient to dispose of the usefulness of the immortality-of-the-soul hypothesis, it remains unclear why the apocalyptic approach, specifically, must therefore be embraced as the only means of discoursing about human yearning for survival beyond death. In fact there appears to be another circular argument at work here, parallel to the one mentioned just now. If one works naturally with apocalyptic categories, then one's concerns about life after death are moulded accordingly. But if – as surely is the case today – such categories are far

from natural, indeed seriously alien, then no amount of philosophising about our fate would seem to require such an interpretation.

In sum, neither of these attempts by Pannenberg in *Jesus – God and Man* to legitimate an apocalyptic interpretation seems compelling. However, he retains two, more deep-seated, convictions which he offers in favour of his construction. The first, a theological argument, goes right to the heart of his concern to foster the apologetic strength of theology and to dismiss what he regards as the 'arbitrary' features of dialectical theology. For this reason he maintains that:

> a splitting up of historical consciousness into a detection of facts and an evaluation of them . . . is intolerable to Christian faith . . . because the message of the resurrection of Jesus and of God's revelation in him necessarily becomes merely subjective interpretation.[55]

In short, it is claimed, such a split is 'theologically impossible', for the result is that faith is reduced to mere 'enthusiasm'[56] instead of being soundly based in knowledge. But of course it is this very assertion of the Resurrection's sound basis in knowledge that we are calling into question. If the soundness is not confirmed, the appeal to these theological considerations naturally loses its edge.

The second conviction is Pannenberg's reiteration of his objection to the 'positivistic' historical method which, he claims, 'is based on the futile aim . . . to ascertain bare facts without meaning in history'.[57] However, the question emerges: does this realisation render *any* distinction between fact and appraisal useless, and, further, does this general criticism of the positivists actually help Pannenberg towards his goal? (For he is still primarily concerned with demonstrating that a first-century apocalyptic interpretation is the only appropriate one for the Resurrection texts.) There are two main rejoinders to Pannenberg here; both employ results we have already achieved, and both turn out to highlight further latent tensions in Pannenberg's position.

First, he is surely right to insist that no history is written from an absolutely objective standpoint:[58] all historians bring to their work a set of relatively conscious or unconscious assumptions which duly affect their presentation. But this factor (which indeed implies that there are no such things as 'bare facts') is not of course to be confused with the quite separate proposition that historical events should be interpreted exactly as they were by people of their time. To be sure, in any given generation certain interpretations will tend to be linked with certain facts but, as we have already seen, that is not to say that *past* interpretations have to be ours, even though the original interpretation is something historians will be interested in considering as the evidence is reviewed. In short, though Pannenberg is right about 'bare facts', he would be wrong to use the anti-positivist argument if he meant to bar *any* distinction between fact and interpretation. For the very fact, as Pannenberg himself admits, that every new generation must rewrite history in its own way implies at least a distinction in principle between the original 'fact' and its subsequent and varied interpretations.[59] Actually, we have already seen that Pannenberg would not wish to deny this with regard to historical work generally; but we now find that the exception he makes over the Resurrection involves him in an apparent self-contradiction: on the one hand he chides the positivists for their faith in an 'objective stance' immune from change; on the other he straightaway claims that in the case of the Resurrection, only *one* interpretation can be the appropriate one.

A second rejoinder will reveal another ambiguity. In the case of the Resurrection the 'appropriate' interpretation according to Pannenberg involves, as we have seen, a number of theological assertions which are by no means uncontentious. Therefore historians in this one instance, whatever their religious affiliation, are seemingly required to assent to the existence of the God of the Hebrew Scriptures and to that God's personal revelation in this act of raising up Jesus. There is an obvious oddity in this argument, however, for the *reductio ad absurdum* is that avowedly atheist or agnostic historians would in this case be in an imponderable dilemma as to how to perform their proper roles as historians. But Pannenberg has another claim of even wider implications. In the context of a discussion about universal history, which also has the Resurrection as its clue, he goes so far as to say that:

> A radical humanism, which would understand all events as nothing but life expressions of man, must lose sight of the specifically historical.[60]

In short, the concept of God is allegedly indispensable if historians are to do their job properly at any time, not just where the Resurrection is concerned.

It is, of course, Pannenberg's dogged refusal to acknowledge what is simply accepted practice amongst secular historians that perplexes and puzzles here. *Prima facie*, they are not likely to be impressed by his insistence that what they are *really* presupposing in their work (subconsciously at least) is that God is the creator and sustainer of all history. But we have, by now, unpeeled the intricate layers of argumentation that allowed Pannenberg at the time of *Jesus – God and Man* to arrive at this apparently paradoxical conclusion. We have seen how a certain degree of 'muddle' in his discussion of historical analogy permitted him to slide into a discussion of the Resurrection without the relevant degree of caution appropriate to examination of a supposed 'law violation'. We also detected some further muddles in the reasoning attending his evaluation of the detailed evidence concerning Jesus' Resurrection. We now see, however, how fundamental to Pannenberg's *interpretation* of the Resurrection is the underlying appeal to an anthropological constant – the human hope beyond death.[61] If he fails to establish such a constant, the interpretative framework crumbles, the theistic underpinnings become insecure.

But it is precisely in this area – that of supporting bulwarks for theism founded in anthropology – that Pannenberg's thought has most significantly developed since the time of *Jesus – God and Man*.[62] The systematic import of such a development seems, correspondingly, to allow less dangerous weight to fall on a successful verification of theistic action in the one, 'historical' event of Jesus' Resurrection.[63]

107

A similar shift has been evident in British analytic philosophy of religion since the early 1970s. What was a direct riposte to the sceptic on the 'miraculous' in Richard Swinburne's *Concept of Miracle* (1970), for instance, broadened out into a new 'inductive' approach to the arguments for God's existence *tout court*.[64] Thus the apolgetic strategy became more subtle and diffuse: one could now scarcely hope to convince the non-believer of theism by appeal to the 'miraculous' alone; rather, a 'cumulative case' for theism needed to be made first, and only then the assessment of the Resurrection done in the light of an assumed theistic perspective. This shift of strategy is, of course, crucial for what we earlier called the 'burden of proof' issue. If Christian theism (and, with that, cases of 'miraculous intervention') can already be presumed by the historical investigator when the evidence for Jesus' Resurrection is evaluated, then much follows; it is not that the evidence *per se* is strengthened, but rather that the degree of scepticism normally accorded to a 'law violation' is duly tempered. The 'background evidence', as Swinburne calls it, provides one with a significant impetus to assess the fragmentary evidence in a more positive way.[65]

Where, then, has this discussion led us? It would seem that, in the area of the 'miraculous' considered alone, a hardnosed riposte to the logical positivist in philosophy, or the historical positivist in historiography, was a 'strategy of the brave' characteristic of the late 1960s and early 1970s. It was, however, a minority taste even then, the dominant theological trend, as we saw, being to veer away from direct engagement with the sceptic altogether. The task of my argument has been to show that that hard-nosed strategy was fallible; for, if I am right, this head-on engagement with secular historiographical method can, in the case of the Resurrection, lead us only as far as an impasse, an elusive question mark.

But this is where the issue of 'mystery', as opposed to sheer 'muddle', begins interestingly to obtrude; for the very nature of that question mark may be theologically significant for Resurrection faith. Moreover, what is fascinating about Pannenberg's discussion at points in *Jesus – God and Man* (and indeed elsewhere), is that he also admits this – in a way at least potentially destabilising to the other components of his argument. This will be the last feature of his position that we must examine briefly, for it has important systematic implications.

We have so far concentrated on those (dominant) elements in Pannenberg's case for the Resurrection in which he concentrates on making his arguments completely respectable in the eyes of secular historians and scientists alike. This makes him dismissive of any suggestion that the Resurrection is not 'historical' in the sense of having an objective reality, placed in the normal time continuum.[66] At moments, too, he can even flatten out the claim to the 'miraculous', in the Humean sense, by an apparent sleight of hand: he hints that the 'transformation' of Jesus' body in the Resurrection might not, strictly, be a violation of 'law' from the perspective of the *eschaton*; if this 'transformation' is, as Paul held, the goal of all Christians (1 Corinthians 15), then it cannot ultimately be perceived as a 'non-repeatable violation' (to use Swinburne's language).[67] But the other side of Pannenberg's rhetoric here is the surprising stress on the utter *unknowability* of what we seek to grasp and describe in Jesus' Resurrection. Thus he can swing to assert that 'we are dealing with a transformation into a reality which is *entirely unknown* to us'.[68] More strangely still, he can argue thus in *Jesus – God and Man*.

> The intended reality [of Resurrection] is beyond the experience of the man who lives on this side of death. Thus the only possible way of speaking about it is metaphorical, using images of this-worldly occurrences. *Anyone who has become conscious of this structure involved in speaking about resurrection from the dead can no longer fancy that he knows what is thus expressed in the same way that one knows an occurrence that has been investigated scientifically.*[69]

The admission made here is decidedly odd, and seemingly self-defeating. If we are really 'unable to know *at all* what the expression "resurrection of the dead" ... means',[70] as Pannenberg says at one point, then how can the carefully nuanced historical arguments, described above, lead us to the conclusion that Jesus' 'Resurrection' has indeed occurred? Even more bemusingly, how can we have the well-founded confidence that the final event will not bring anything decisively new that was not already anticipated in the Resurrection of Jesus[71] when the content of this anticipated faith is so obscure? If Pannenberg wants the Resurrection to be 'historical', it must, at least, have some indicable noetic *content.* But it is precisely this that appears to be in question.

It would be tempting to see this strand of Pannenberg's argument as a final and fatal flaw – a failure in both consistency and coherence. But instead, I am inclined to be indulgent:[72] the language of 'mystery', and the appeal of 'metaphor', from one otherwise profoundly opposed to subjectivity, obfuscation, or fideism, is a signal of something important occurring, albeit inadequately expressed by Pannenberg himself. For if indeed the Resurrection of Jesus *was* a 'proleptic' anticipation of the final end, as 1 Corinthians 15 also insists, then we might well expect an element of forward-looking mystery and anticipation, a failure fully to contain the meaning of the event in currently-known categories.[73] And this, indeed, may be precisely why the Resurrection, historically considered, does, and even should, end with the elusive question mark we spoke of above. To have arrived at this point is not necessarily to dive into a realm of dangerously subjective *eisegesis,* as Pannenberg himself fears.[74] Rather, it is to start another (perfectly objective) discussion, which unfortunately goes beyond the confines of this present essay: a discussion of the phenomenology, theological complexity, and symbolic density of the experience of 'Resurrection' in the New Testament and later tradition.[75] But this is the point at which the focus on the 'Resurrection' *qua* 'historical' transformation of Jesus' post-mortem body is necessarily transcended.

Conclusions

I must now sum up my conclusions. This essay has had a modest set of tasks and goals to pursue. It has been written in full agreement with Pannenberg (and against a major tide of theological opinion) that clarity about the 'historical' status of Jesus' Resurrection is an apologetic necessity for any serious-minded Christian. But it has criticised Pannenberg, at times severely, for 'muddles' created by an overzealous attempt to validate the Resurrection's 'historicity' in the terms of secular historiography and science. If such 'historical' arguments are to convince, I argued, then a theistic background must already be presupposed, and that wider task is one that has indeed much exercised Pannenberg in the interim years since writing *Jesus – God and Man*. Even then, the conclusions we may reach when considering the Resurrection as a strictly 'historical' matter may be fragmentary and elusive. The element of 'mystery' in the Resurrection is something we have treated only briefly in Pannenberg – but sympathetically, despite his ostensible self-contradiction in this area. Were analytic philosophers of religion now to apply their recent insights into the nature of 'metaphor'[76] to these wider dimensions of Resurrection belief, significant developments could occur in a debate that otherwise has settled into rather predictable contours since the time of the original publication of *Jesus – God and Man*.[77] Such an interaction between continental theology and Anglo-American philosophy of religion would be a welcome development indeed, and could illuminate the Resurrection's 'mystery' without endangering the elements of 'muddle' we have here sought to expose.

Notes

1 For Barth, see esp. K. Barth, *The Resurrection of the Dead* (Eng. tr., London: Hodder and Stoughton, 1933); for Bultmann, see in particular ed. H. Bartsch, *Kerygma and Myth*, I (Eng. tr. of vols I and II, London: SPCK, 1972), 1–44. The two differ on whether the Resurrection must be seen as an 'objective' (albeit extraordinary) event or not, but agree that it cannot be constrained within the categories of 'history'. For discussion of the dominance of this trend against regarding the Resurrection as 'historical' in mid-twentieth-century theology see P. Carnley, *The Structure of Resurrection Belief* (Oxford: OUP, 1987 esp. chs 1 and 3).

2 D. Hume, 'Of Miracles', from *An Enquiry Concerning Human Understanding*, section x, reprinted in ed. R. Wollheim, *Hume on Religion* (London: Collins, 1963), 224.

3 Eng. tr. of *Grundzüge der Christologie* (Gütersloh: Gerd Mohn, 1964), as *Jesus – God and Man* (London: SCM, 1968).

4 W. Pannenberg, *The Apostles' Creed* (Eng. tr., London: SCM, 1972), 97.

5 Consider, e.g., the relieved appeal to Pannenberg on the resurrection p. 53, ed. M. Green, *The Truth of God Incarnate* (London: Hodder and Stoughton, 1977); the conservative riposte to ed. J. Hick, *The Myth of God Incarnate* (London: SCM, 1977).

6 Amongst relevant secondary articles to date we may mention, in order of appearance: H. Burhenn, 'Pannenberg's Argument for the Historicity of the Resurrection', *Journal of the American Academy of Religion*, 40, 1972, 368–79; T. Peters, 'Jesus' Resurrection: An Historical Event without Analogy', *Dialog*, 12, 1973, 112–16; G.E. Michalson, 'Pannenberg on the Resurrection and Historical Method', *Scottish Journal of Theology*, 33, 1980, 345–59; E. Johnson, 'Resurrection and Reality in the Thought of Wolfhart Pannenberg', *Heythrop Journal*, 24, 1983, 1–18; W.L. Craig, 'Pannenberg's Beweis für die Auferstehung Jesu', *Kerygma und Dogma*, 34, 1988, 78–104. Eds. C.E. Braaten and P. Clayton, *The Theology of Wolfhart Pannenberg* (Minneapolis, MN: Augsburg, 1988) contains useful biography of secondary material and an appraisal of the literature by S.J. Grenz (pp. 19–52).

7 Vol II of Pannenberg's *Systematische Theologie* was frustratingly still unavailable in Oxford libraries at the time of the final revision of this essay. Vol. I (Göttingen: Vandenhoeck and Ruprecht, 1988) is available in Eng. tr.: *Systematic Theology* (Edinburgh: T and T Clark, 1991).

8 For such a range, see again eds. Braaten and Clayton (see n. 6); and, before that, A.D. Galloway, *Wolfhart Pannenberg* (London: Allen and Unwin, 1973), E.F. Tupper, *The Theology of Wolfhart Pannenberg* (Philadelphia, 1973), D. McKenzie *Wolfhart Pannenberg and Religious Philosophy* (Washington, D.C.: University Press of America, 1980).

9 For relevant features of Swinburne's programme see esp. R. Swinburne, *The Concept of Miracle* (London: Macmillan, 1970), idem, *The Existence of God* (Oxford: OUP, 1979), esp. ch. 12, and idem, *Revelation* (Oxford, 1991) esp. ch. 7.

10 *The Apostles' Creed*, 97 (my italics).

11 *Jesus – God and Man*, 97.

12 R.G. Collingwood, *The Idea of History* (Oxford: OUP, 1946), 240.

13 W. Pannenberg, *Basic Questions in Theology* (Eng. tr. 3 vols, London: SCM, 1970, 1971, 1973): vol. I, 47.

14 Ibid. 43f. Pannenberg uses Ernst Troeltsch as his exemplar of this 'positivist' stance. This is unfortunate, since the quotations are taken from a short early essay of Troeltsch's (and arguably distort his meaning). His mature position on analogy is certainly not subject to the same criticism (cf. E. Troeltsch, *Gesammelte Schriften* III (Tübingen, 1922), 190f.)

15 F.H. Bradley 'The Presuppositions of Critical History', in *Collected Essays*, Vol. I (Oxford: OUP, 1935), 24.

16 Whilst Van A Harvey might not on other grounds be dubbed a 'positivist', he seems to display a tendency in this direction when he remarks
about the Resurrection, 'There are no criteria for dealing with an
event unlike any other. We simply do not know what would "count for"
an absolutely unique event.' (*The Historian and the Believer* (London:
SCM, 1967), 228–9.) A similar point was made by Don Cupitt, *Christ
and the Hiddenness of God* (London: Lutterworth, 1971), 139f.

17 *Basic Questions*, vol. I, 46 (my italics).

18 London: Macmillan, 1970.

19 *Hume on Religion*, 208f.

20 Hume himself is notoriously mixed on this point. He leaves room, at
least, for such a positive account, and this is the line pursued by
Swinburne. But the dominant tone of his essay 'Of Miracles' is almost
dogmatically sceptical.

21 Swinburne refines his argument slightly in the later *Existence of God* so
as to admit that 'violations' of statistically founded 'laws' can only
properly be called 'quasi-violations' (ibid. 321–2).

22 *The Concept of Miracle*, 27. In conversation Swinburne admits that the
crucial factors here are the unpredictability and inexplicability of
the violation; in principle, that is, it *could* happen again.

23 *Hume on Religion*, 206.

24 Ibid. 211.

25 See esp. *The Concept of Miracle*, 58–9.

26 *Jesus – God and Man*, 105.

27 Ibid. 94.

28 Ibid. 93.

29 One might also add that any formal distinction here was probably a
temporal one, to the effect that only the disciples and their supporters
in Jerusalem *at the beginning* were those who really experienced the
Resurrected Christ. This would give them a peculiar authority (1 Corinthians 9:1, 2 Corinthians 12:11) to which Paul aspires also in his desire
to show that his experience was of the same quality (1 Corinthians
15:8–9). In the Lucan theology, the Ascension is another way of design-
ating a temporal break of this sort (Luke 24:11, Acts 1:9).

30 *Jesus – God and Man*, 96.

31 Ibid. (my italics).

32 Ibid. 96.

33 Ibid. 95 (my italics).

34 Ibid. 101.

35 Ibid. 100.

36 Ibid. 103.

37 Ibid. 105.

38 Ibid. 101.

39 Ibid. 105.

40 Ibid. 89.

41 J.A.T. Robinson, *The Human Face of God* (London: SCM, 1973), 132.

113

42 Strangely, in *The Apostles' Creed* Pannenberg would seem to share Hume's attitude to the burden of proof when he advises us to be 'suspicious' of an event that 'stands in contradiction to otherwise well-formulated assumptions' (111); scepticism, he says, is the appropriate attitude (112). But on the very next page (113) the burden of proof seem to have shifted back again. There he states that, 'all attempts to explain the appearance of the risen Jesus as hallucinations have failed. . . The necessary indicators are lacking. . .'

43 See *Jesus – God and Man*, 97–8.

44 Ibid. 73.

45 *Basic Questions*, vol. 1, 106 (my italics).

46 In: eds. J.M. Robinson and J.B. Cobb, *Theology as History* (New York: Harper and Row, 1967), 127; cf. also 247 n. 46.

47 For extended dicussion of hermeneutics in Pannenberg's earlier work, see esp. *Basic Questions*, vol. 1, 1–14: 'The Crisis of the Scripture Principle'; 96–136: 'Hermeneutic and Universal History'; 137–181: 'On Historical and Theological Hermeneutics'; and *Basic Questions*, vol. III, 192–210: 'Eschatology and the Experience of Meaning'.

48 *Jesus – God and Man*, 81.

49 Ibid. 83–5. See also W Pannenberg, *What is Man?* (Philadelphia: Fortress Press, 1970), esp. ch. 1.

50 *Jesus – God and Man*, 84.

51 Ibid. 83.

52 See ibid., 79.

53 *Basic Questions*, vol. 1, 176.

54 *Jesus – God and Man*, 87 (my italics). See also W. Pannenberg *et al. Revelation as History* (Toronto: Macmillan, 1968), 148.

55 *Theology as History*, 126.

56 *Basic Questions*, vol. II, 66. See also ibid. 81–91; 'Kerygma and History, *passim*.

57 *Theology as History*, 126.

58 Christopher Blake, whose article 'Can History be Objective' has become something of a classic (originally in *Mind* for 1955; now in: ed. P. Gardiner, *Theories of History* (London: Allen and Unwin, 1959), 329–43), points out that this idea of *absolute* objectivity in historical work is an impossible ideal, and usually merely confuses discussion. See 331–2.

59 To be fair to Pannenberg, he does occasionally acknowledge that some such distinction between fact and meaning is implied by his own hermeneutical method; see *Theology as History*, 272, n. 87.

60 *Basic Questions*, vol. I, 76.

61 Thus at one point he specifically says that he does not intend that we should 'infer' the existence of God directly from a specific historical event (*Theology as History*, 255), rather the question of God is already present because of the very nature of the human.

62 See the helpful discussion of Pannenberg's more recent developments

by C. Schwöbel in ed. D.F. Ford, *The Modern Theologians* (Oxford: Blackwell, 1989), ch. 13, esp. 272, 283. Also see W Pannenberg, *Theology and the Philosophy of Science* (Eng. tr., London: DLT, 1976), esp. ch. 5; and *Systematic Theology*, vol. 1, esp. chs 2 and 3.

63 See ibid. 283, and W Pannenberg's *Systematic Theology*, vol. 1, 56–7.

64 See *The Existence of God*, and the place of ch. 12, 'Arguments from History and Miracles', within it.

65 See R. Swinburne, *Revelation*, 112f.

66 See, e.g., *Jesus – God and Man*, 99; *The Apostles' Creed*, 114.

67 For this strain of argument see *The Apostles' Creed*, 97–9. (This point emerged more clearly still in private correspondence of 1963 between Pannenberg and Gordon D. Kaufman of Harvard. Professor Kaufman kindly allowed me to see these letters, but it would be inappropriate to quote them here without Professor Pannenberg's explicit permission).

68 *The Apstoles' Creed*, 98 (my italics).

69 *Jesus – God and Man*, 75 (my italics).

70 *Basic Questions*, vol. I, 24 (my ialics).

71 *Basic Questions*, vol. II, 44.

72 Compare my approach here to that of Michaelson (n. 6), who takes Pannenberg's inconsistency on this point to be fatal. Surely all that has happened here is that Pannenberg has overstated his case: his 'positive' understanding of 'analogy' (see my first section *supra*) allows him to stretch imaginatively from the known to the unknown; but it is the occasional claim that we can know or say *nothing* of the content of the Resurrection belief that bemuses.

73 This dimension of mystery is strangely lacking from Swinburne's understanding of the meaning of the Resurrection (Revelation, ch. 7), despite his own nuanced understanding of the meaning of the 'metaphorical' (ibid. ch. 3).

74 See, e.g., *Basic Questions*, vol. II, 44.

75 Amongst recent literature on the topic, see again esp. Carnley's work (n. 1), *passim*.

76 See esp. (from very different theological and ideological standpoints), J.M. Soskice, *Metaphor and Religious Language* (Oxford: OUP, 1985) and R. Swinburne, *Revelation*, esp. ch. 3.

77 So, for instance, G. Habermas and A. Flew, ed. T. Miethe *Did Jesus Rise from the Dead?* (San Francisco: Harper and Row, 1987), which includes a contribution from Pannenberg (125–35), retreads the familiar ground we have explored between sceptic and apologist. Carnley's *The Structure of Resurrection Belief*, imaginative in contrast, is on the other hand strikingly unconnected with the philosophy of religion discussion about the miraculous.

7. The Resurrection and the Empty Tomb*

Barnabas Lindars, SSF

The crucial question

The empty tomb is for many people the decisive factor for Resurrection faith. Here we have an observable, physical phenomenon. It is described in all four Gospels, and there seems to be no reason to doubt it. Not only is there the testimony of the women (or of Mary Magdalene alone, according to John 20:1–18), but there is a further tradition that Peter visited the tomb in response to their message and found it empty (Luke 24:12, cf. John 20:3–10).[1]

So the empty tomb provides strong evidence for the *fact* of the Resurrection. The one who died and was buried is the one whom 'God raised up, having loosed the pangs of death, because it was not possible for him to be held by it' (Acts 2:24). Of course, other explanations are possible. Some people have thought that the women made a mistake and went to the wrong tomb, though Peter's visit surely excludes this suggestion. In John 20:3, 13, 15, Mary Magdalene imagines that the body of Jesus has been taken away by someone. This reflects the explanation, which became current among Jews, that the disciples themselves stole the body and disposed of it elsewhere in order to claim that Jesus was risen (Matthew 27:62–64; 28:11–15). But this is frankly incredible in view of the moral earnestness and burning conviction which lies behind the earliest Christian preaching. The Gospel could perhaps have been influenced by an inspired misunderstanding of the truth, but it is most

* © The estate of the late Barnabas Lindars 1993

improbable that it depends upon a deliberate deception. If doubt is cast on the veracity of the empty tomb stories, it is for better reasons than these.

The empty tomb is also felt to be decisive for the idea of the *bodily resurrection* of Jesus. The fact of the Resurrection is supported by the accounts of the appearances of Jesus, which go beyond the Gospels and include the very important tradition used by Paul in 1 Corinthians 15:4–7. But the appearance stories by themselves are ambiguous where bodily resurrection is concerned. Apparently, Jesus can pass through locked doors (John 20:19, 26) and disappear at will (Luke 24:31). The disciples think they are seeing a 'spirit', and Jesus has to invite them to handle him, and even eats in front of them, to show that he is real (Luke 24:36–43). He also points to his wounded hands and feet (Luke 24:39; cf. John 20:20, 25–27). The theme of doubt is surprisingly frequent in the appearance stories (cf. Matthew 28:16; Mark 16:11, 13, 14 in the longer ending of Mark;[2] Luke 24:25, 37–38, 41; John 20:25, 27, 29). Thus it was apparently impossible to be sure that Jesus had risen bodily from the tomb on the evidence of the appearances alone. Though we shall have cause to give a different interpretation of the evidence in what follows, the fact remains that for very many modern readers the doctrine of the bodily resurrection of Jesus is inextricably linked with the historicity of the empty tomb.

Thirdly, the empty tomb has something to tell about *our own destiny.* Paul, in 1 Corinthians 15, argues that the ultimate destiny of those who belong to Christ will be a bodily resurrection comparable with that of Christ himself. He is careful to explain that the decomposition of the body does not affect this, because the resurrection body is a matter of being newly clothed with a spiritual body, not subject to mortality and corruption. He relates this to the bodily resurrection of Jesus by means of his metaphor of the first fruits (1 Corinthians 15:20, 23). In the light of Paul's argument it is possible to think of the risen body of Jesus as a transformed body. This goes far to explaining the difficulties just mentioned about the fleeting character of Jesus' body in the appearance stories.

117

For all these reasons the story of the empty tomb is widely held to be the crucial evidence for the historical fact of the Resurrection. To cast doubt on it is felt to undermine the central doctrine of Christianity. That also means rejecting the historical value of the New Testament, or at least treating it in a cavalier fashion in which each scholar decides what is historical and what is unhistorical, leaving the non-specialist confused and unhappy. But the empty tomb story is too important to be dismissed lightly. There is thus a very strong motive for retaining the historicity of this tradition in spite of all difficulties, and those who take the opposite course are viewed with the gravest suspicion.

Method of study

The purpose of this chapter is to put this crucial question into another perspective, which I hope will be found to be supportive of Resurrection faith rather than destructive. I shall argue that it is a mistake to lay such emphasis on the historical value of the empty tomb stories. The fact of the Resurrection, and its character as bodily resurrection, are not argued on the basis of the empty tomb in Paul's argument in 1 Corinthians 15, but that chapter makes a far better basis for Resurrection faith. It also points to the real factors which lie behind the original proclamation of the Resurrection. Further study of the Resurrection traditions will show that the empty tomb stories form part of a larger tendency to rationalise the faith of the Resurrection at a stage for the most part later than Paul. Thus, so far from being the origin of belief in the Resurrection, the empty tomb stories arose from this belief. This explains why they were apparently unknown to Paul.

The point which needs to be clearly understood at the outset is that any attmept to make sense of the Resurrection traditions is a process of rationalisation. It is not a matter of explaining away the Resurrection, so as to avoid uncomfortable conclusions. The question whether a miracle was involved in the Resurrection is really a red herring. Salvation in any sense is a miracle, the triumph of God over the forces of evil, destruction and death. The Gospels, relying on oral traditions, indicate the saving effect of Jesus' ministry by recounting miracle stories. But it is not to be supposed that salvation in its deepest sense was confined to those whose limbs were restored to health and whose eyes were made capable of sight. The presentation of such miracle traditions, particularly in Mark and John, is clearly geared to point to their deeper significance in relation to universal well-being and to sight in the sense of understanding of the truth. It is very likely that the miracle stories gained currency as popular modes of expressing these aspects of the impact of Jesus on his audience. How far they have a factual basis is impossible to determine. The ministry of Jesus took place among people who were ready to believe in miracles, and miracle stories are told of other teachers at this time, such as Hanina ben Dosa and Honi the Circle-Drawer. Similarly, the Resurrection stories, including the accounts of the empty tomb, belong to a popular strand of oral tradition. They express the truths of the Gospel through vivid incidents. From this point of view they can be seen to be rationalisations of the Resurrection faith among people for whom abstract truths tend to be expressed in concrete forms.

The Resurrection stories circulated first among Jewish people who already had a belief in personal resurrection expressed in pictorial ways. Hence, the empty tomb and other stories did not cause a jolt to their basic understanding, but could be accommodated within it. For some of Paul's converts at Corinth, however, this was not the case. Paul reports that they 'say that there is no resurrection of the dead' (1 Corinthians 15:12). He has to convince them on their own terms. His argument in this great chapter is, then, another example of rationalisation, which is notable for his treatment of the concept of the resurrection body.

Modern study of the Resurrection traditions is also a process of rationalisation, whether the student is a believer or not. Those who cling to the historicity of the empty tomb rationalise the sources just as much as the most detached and sceptical scholars. They take the accounts in the Gospels at face value, which (as just pointed out) may be a distortion of their true evidential character. They furthermore cannot

119

avoid harmonising the different presentations in the various Gospels because of the glaring inconsistencies. Did the women say nothing to anyone, as Mark 16:8 asserts, or did they duly pass on the angel's message to the Apostles, as is claimed in Luke 24:10? Did they meet with the Risen Jesus himself as they returned from the tomb, as stated in Matthew 28:8–10, or did no one see him, as reported by the two disciples in Luke 24:22–24? Perhaps these contradictions are not significant, as no two people's accounts of the same incidents are ever exactly the same. But the reader has to form some kind of a judgement on the sources, and a measure of harmonisation, which is one form of rationalisation, is inevitable. Then a further rationalising procedure is likely to take place when the implications of the facts thus deduced are made the basis for personal Resurrection faith.

Modern scholarship starts from the fact that the stories are contained in written documents, and therefore subjects them to literary analysis. This requires different methods, depending on the purpose which the analysis is intended to serve. If the aim is to establish the historical value of a tradition, the various tools of historical criticism must be brought into action. These include source criticism to establish the relationship between the Gospel accounts, form criticism to identify their social function in the community in the underlying oral stage of transmission, and redaction criticism to establish the tendencies of the different Evangelists in the way they have presented them. It is also necessary to compare them with such historical evidence as may be preserved outside the Gospels. From this point of view the letters of Paul have special importance, partly because he wrote them before any of the four Gospels reached their present form, but chiefly because he has preserved a formal statement concerning the Resurrection which he received from the Jerusalem Church, probably from Peter himself (1 Corinthians 15:3–7).

Other scholarly approaches, such as structural analysis, are concerned with the literary character of the Resurrection stories as they stand in the text, regardless of their synoptic relationships and their historical value. These are valuable

120

for exposing the dynamics of the stories and the ideas which they are intended to convey, but lead away from the historical problems which, I have suggested, are for many people crucially important in deciding whether it is true that Jesus rose from the dead. It is with these problems that we shall now be concerned.

Jewish ideas of resurrection

The Resurrection of Jesus was not a bombshell that exploded among people with no previous concept of personal resurrection. On the contrary, most Jews had some belief in resurrection (apart from the well-known case of the Sadducees), and it is taken for granted in the teaching of Jesus himself. Contemporary Jewish ideas of resurrection are known from various sources, and provide the essential basis for understanding the New Testament doctrine. The idea of a general resurrection appears in the Bible in the later part of Daniel, which is generally dated shortly after 164 BC. It is significant that it is described in material fashion: 'Many of those who sleep in the dust of the earth shall awake, some to everlasting life, and some to shame and everlasting contempt' (12:2). Nothing is said of the state of the dead during the time before the end. Other Jewish apocalyptic books give more detail. 1 Enoch 22, which may be a little earlier than Daniel, describes Enoch's spiritual journey through the heavens. On the way he sees the souls of the dead awaiting the general resurrection. They are divided into four classes in accordance with the merits of their earthly life; the righteous are in a place of light, whereas the rest are in places of darkness. Thus, while their bodies sleep in the earth, their souls are in a place of waiting until soul and body are reunited at the general resurrection. This picture is reflected in 2 Esdras (4 Ezra), which belongs to the late first century AD. Here 'the souls of the righteous who are in their chambers ask . . . "How long are we to remain here? And when will come the harvest of our reward?" ' (4:35). They are told that it will be until 'the number of those like yourselves is completed' (4:36). Later on Ezra is told about the general

121

resurrection: 'The earth shall give up those who are asleep in it, and the dust those who dwell silently in it; and the chambers shall give up the souls which have been committed to them' (7:32).

These ideas were not just the property of the apocalyptic writers, but were held in various forms by many Jews in the New Testament period. They were especially promoted by the Pharisees in their concern to raise the standard of fidelity to the Law and the pursuit of moral righteousness among the common people. The teaching of Jesus is quite similar. Referring to the general resurrection, he suggests that the new life will not be the same as earthly life, in which people are married, but a life comparable to the existence of the angels (Mark 12:25). He also produces an argument for the continuing existence of the souls in readiness for the general resurrection from God's self-designation as the God of Abraham, Isaac and Jacob (Mark 12:26–27, quoting Exodus. 3:6): 'He is not God of the dead, but of the living.' In the parable of the rich man and Lazarus it is probable that Abraham's bosom is intended to be one of the places of waiting, whereas the rich man is in another place of waiting, characterised by fiery torments and separated from the other by an unbridgeable chasm (Luke 16:22–26). The concept of Hades in this parable should not be confused with the later sharp distinction between heaven above and hell beneath.

Another way of looking at the different places of the souls during the waiting period was to think of them as varying in proximity to God himself. This is an especially important concept for the earliest Christian thinking, as we shall see in a moment, but becomes explicit in the New Testament in only one place, Revelation 6:9–11. Here John, seeing into heaven, 'saw under the altar the souls of those who had been slain for the word of God. . . . They cried out with a loud voice, "O sovereign Lord, holy and true, how long before thou wilt judge and avenge our blood?" Then they were . . . told to rest a little longer, until the number of their fellow servants and their brethren should be complete.' The similarity to 2 Esdras 4:35, quoted above, is striking. But the important point is their position under the altar, for this is the nearest possible place to God. This is illuminated by a saying attributed to Rabbi Akiba (died AD 135) in 'Aboth of Rabbi Nathan' 26: 'Whoever was buried in the land of Israel was just as if he was buried under the altar, and whoever was buried under the altar was just as if he was buried under the throne of glory.' Less specific, but reflecting roughly contemporary views, is the report of Justin, writing about AD 135, of the opinion of an elderly Jewish-Christian that 'The souls of the pious remain in a better place, while those of the unjust and wicked are in a worse, waiting for the time of judgement' ('Dialogue' 5).

Finally, we should note that the bodily aspect of resurrection is often represented as the awakening of those who sleep in the graves (Daniel 12:2; 2 Esdras 7:32; 2 Baruch 50:2; 4 Baruch 6:6–10; 1 Enoch 61:1; 'Apocalypse of Moses' 41; 'Pseudo-Phocylides' 103–104; 'Testament of Judah' 25:4). This does not necessarily imply disregard of the decomposition of the body, for Ezekiel's vision of the reconstitution of people from dry bones (Ezekiel 37:1–14) was applied to the future general resurrection in the 'Lives of the Prophets' 3:12 (probably written in the early first century AD), and subsequently in rabbinic literature and in the frescoes of the synagogue of Dura-Europos. Thus what was intended as a metaphor is taken as prophecy of the end time. Isaiah 26:1 could be understood similarly. But the most striking expression of this idea is found in a Jewish-Christian tradition included by Matthew in connection with the rending of the temple at the moment of Christ's death: 'The earth shook, and the rocks were split; the tombs also were opened, and many bodies of the saints who had fallen asleep were raised, and coming out of the tombs after his resurrection, they went into the holy city and appeared to many' (Matthew 27:51–53). The point is that, with the cataclysmic event of the death of Jesus, the final upheavals which presage the general resurrection have begun, and the bodies already start to rise from their graves. We shall have to return to this passage later. The joining of body and soul at the general resurrection is rarely mentioned apart from 2 Esdras 7:32,

123

but is argued on the basis of the famous parable of the lame man and the blind man in the 'Apocryphon of Ezekiel': just as the lame man provides the eyes and the blind man the legs, and so the two act as one man, so body and soul must be judged together at the great assize.[3]

The earliest record

These are some of the ideas which would be in the minds of many Jews who first heard the proclamation of the Resurrection, and of Peter and the other Apostles who first proclaimed it. It is not too much to say that the original experience of the fact of resurrection, whatever that may have been, would be sure to be expressed in the light of this kind of pre-understanding. We must now look at the New Testament evidence from this point of view in the hope of achieving a probable reconstruction of what actually happened and a logical account of the growth of the traditions in connection with it. This will then furnish the basis for an assessment of the stories of the empty tomb.

First, it will be best to look again at 1 Corinthians 15:3–7 in more detail. Paul says explicitly that it is a statement which he has received and subsequently passed on to the converts in Corinth. The most likely occasion when he received it (or it was confirmed, if he originally received it from the Christians in Damascus) would be his visit to Jerusalem three years after his conversion, when he stayed with Cephas (Peter) for a fortnight (Galatians 1:18). Considering the importance of the statement, it is likely that he now reproduces it exactly. Thus we have here an official formulary which can be traced back to the earliest period of the primitive Church, probably less than five years after the Resurrection itself.

The statement begins with the Crucifixion: 'Christ died for our sins according to the scriptures' (15:3). It may be that the designation 'Christ' comes from Paul, replacing 'the Lord Jesus' (cf. 11:23), as he tends to use Christ alone as a name for Jesus throughout this chapter and also frequently elsewhere. However that may be, there can be no doubt that this is a Messianic statement, asserting the fact that Jesus died *as Messiah*, because there is a clear reference to Isaiah 53:5 in the phrase 'for our sins', endorsed by the words 'according to the scriptures'. The need to prove that 'it was necessary for the Christ to suffer' (Acts 17:3) was felt in the earliest days of the Church, and the proof was found in prophecy, especially Isaiah 53.

Next comes the burial: 'that he was buried' (15:4). It is often supposed that this is a hint of the empty tomb story on the grounds that, as a lead into the following statement of the Resurrection, it prepares the reader to think of that as an action which leaves the tomb empty. But this really only makes it more significant that, when it comes to the point, the emptiness of the tomb is not mentioned at all. For the statement of the burial primarily points backwards, underlining the reality of Jesus' death which has just been mentioned. If it is also intended to prepare for the empty tomb in what follows, the reader can only be disappointed. Thus the function of this reference to the burial should be understood as confirmation of the death stated in verse 3.

The statement of the Resurrection exactly balances that on the death: 'that he was raised on the third day in accordance with the scriptures' (15:4). The passive verb is probably an example of the 'divine passive', avoiding direct mention of God, so that it means 'God raised him'. As before, the reference to the scriptures is probably to be taken closely with 'on the third day'. Though it is not so easy to determine the primary scriptures referred to, it must again mean Messianic texts, and most probably texts which include the idea of the third day. This points to Hosea 6:2 (not actually quoted in the New Testament) and Jonah 1:17 (cf. Matthew 12:40). Both are used in connection with the general resurrection in the rabbinic literature. Once more the point of mentioning the scriptures is to assert that Jesus rose as Messiah.

Here it must be pointed out that both statements on death and resurrection have a basis in the words of Jesus himself in addition to the scriptural references. This is clear, even if on good critical grounds we discount the formal predictions

(Matthew 16:21, 17:22–23, 20:17–19 and parallels), which have most probably been shaped in the light of the actual events. The death of Jesus for sins is suggested in Mark 10:45, 14:24; Luke 22:19–20; 1 Corinthians 11:24, and the theme of restoration in three days occurs in the temple saying, which probably has an authentic basis, in Matthew 26:61; Mark 14:58; John 2:19. The application of this saying to the death and Resurrection of Jesus appears in the use of it as a taunt by the bystanders in Matthew 27:40; Mark 15:29.

It can now be seen that resurrection on the third day has a basis in a saying of Jesus about renewal in three days, and is confirmed in scriptural prophecy (1 Corinthians 15:4) applied to Jesus as Messiah. This affirmation therefore does not require a visible event on the third day. The third day is part of the theological statement of resurrection. So when in verse 5 the statement turns to the evidence for the Resurrection there is no suggestion that the appearance to Peter took place on the third day. Nor is it said to have happened in Jerusalem.

Thus at this point we must take seriously the tradition in Mark 16:7 that the first appearance of the Risen Jesus was experienced by Peter in Galilee. The danger to Peter on account of being a Galilean associated with Jesus is referred to in Mark 14:70. It is altogether probable that the disciples who had accompanied Jesus on his mission to Jerusalem fled after his arrest (Mark 14:50) and returned to Galilee. It is also clear that the tradition of the appearance to Peter in Galilee is not an original part of the empty tomb story in Mark 16:1–8, which is far more coherent if it is omitted. This observation is supported by another insertion, which sits awkwardly in its context, in Mark 14:28. Significantly, the present setting of the saying is Jesus' prediction of Peter's denials. In this saying Jesus promises, 'After I am raised up, I will go before you to Galilee.' Thus Galilee is the place where the Risen Jesus is first encountered. For Peter it is an encounter inseparable from his repentance for his failure and his need for the gospel of forgiveness through the sacrificial death of Jesus.

1 Corinthians 15:5–7 gives us the official evidence of the Resurrection series of appearances to individuals and groups. It is likely, though it cannot be proved, that the list is related to the steps whereby the primitive Church came into being. On this view the appearance to Peter (referred to also in Luke 24:34) is fundamental. The next appearance to 'the twelve' marks his gathering of the rest of the apostolic band in Galilee and the formal inauguration of the Church. The assembly of over five hundred would be a rally, also in Galilee, in which as many as possible of the disciples of Jesus are brought together. The appearance to James may be related to his appointment as leader of the Church on account of being the nearest kinsman to Jesus himself (cf. Acts 12:17, 15:13, 21:18; Galatians 1:19, 2:9, 12). Then 'all the apostles' refers to the commissioning of the missionaries (not confined to the twelve) who spearhead the Church's action, possibly including the decision to set up the headquarters in Jerusalem. A connection between appearances and apostolic commissioning is a feature of the Gospel stories (Matthew 28:18–20; Mark 16:14–18; Luke 24:49; John 20:21–23; Acts 1:4–8). Paul adds the appearance to himself (1 Corinthians 15:8), which constituted his own apostolic commissioning (cf. 1 Corinthians 9:1). We do not know whether others would approve of this, or would agree that his experience belonged to the same order as those mentioned in the official list.

It is not within the scope of this essay to consider what sort of appearances are covered by this list. The only eyewitness accounts of such appearances are those of Paul himself, though what he says is all too brief (Galatians 1:15–16), and John on Patmos (Revelation 1:9–20). Both are personal visions (cf. the three accounts of Paul's experience in Acts 9:1–19, 22:4–16, 26:9–18), and the same could apply to the appearances to Peter and to James, but corporate visions are harder to imagine. In any case there can be no doubt that the present reality of Jesus as risen from the dead and exalted as Messiah to God's right hand was vividly experienced in some way at these gatherings of Apostles and disciples.

127

The empty tomb

If the Church began in Galilee and only later moved to Jerusalem, it is easier to see why the empty tomb is not referred to as evidence in 1 Corinthians 15:3–7. But, as pointed out above, it is never used as a basis for proving the Resurrection in the New Testament and appears to have been unknown to Paul, writing at least twenty years after the Crucifixion. Thus the rise of the empty tomb tradition must have been comparatively late, though it was well articulated before Mark wrote his Gospel shortly before or after the fall of Jerusalem in AD 70, another twenty years later. The date could be later still if those who hold to the priority of Matthew are right, because on other grounds a date later than AD 70 for Matthew seems to be required (for example, the fall of the city is probably referred to in 22:7).

It thus looks very unlikely that the Apostles went to the tomb to see if it was empty when they moved back to Jerusalem, and we must try to see why this should be so. There are three possibilities that can account for it. Firstly, because of their conviction of the Resurrection derived from their experiences in Galilee, they had no interest in visiting the tomb (cf. Luke 24:5: 'Why do you seek the living among the dead?'). Secondly, because of their flight to Galilee, they had no certain information about the burial-place of Jesus, and eventually they settled for the empty and unused tomb associated with a prominent man named Joseph of Arimathea, which happened to be close to the site of the Crucifixion. Thirdly, they were able to get reliable information from friends in Jerusalem about the burial-place, including perhaps the part played by Joseph, but visits to the tomb did not entail removing the stone and looking inside.

The first suggestion seems to be excluded by the mention of the burial in 1 Corinthians 15:4. But, although I have expressed myself in favour of the second possibility above in a previous article on the subject, I now feel that the same mention of the burial excludes this suggestion as well, as it would be strange to include this detail in the statement if the burial of Jesus was in fact unknown. This leaves the third as the best solution, and it makes good sense in relation to Jewish factors which have already come to our notice.

In the first place, it would be exceptional to open up a tomb unless there were very special circumstances, because contact with the dead incurs seven-day uncleanness (Numbers 19:16; Mishnah Oholoth 1:1). This is disregarded in the story of Lazarus (John 11:39), but the opening of the tomb is obviously exceptional. In normal circumstances a tomb would not be opened until it was needed for a further burial, and then the bones of previous corpses would be moved into a smaller compartment or placed in an ossuary. Gatherings at a tomb to be near the mortal remains of a loved one and to show respect to that person's memory would be held outside the entrance (cf. Mishnah Erubin 5:1 for special chambers for the purpose in large tombs; Mishnah Oholoth 7:1 for booths attached to a tomb).

Secondly, the primary conviction with regard to Jesus is that, being God's designated Messiah, he has been raised to the right hand of God, and this is what is signified in the appearances (cf., besides Paul in 1 Corinthians 15:8 and John in Revelation 1:9–14, the vision attributed to Stephen in Acts 7:55–56). Thus, from the point of view of the time of waiting before the general resurrection, his soul has been raised beyond such an elevated position as the souls of the martyrs under the altar (Revelation 6:9–11) to a place of equality with God himself. This explains Paul's wish in Philippians 1:23: he wants 'to depart and be with Christ', because as one who has been baptised into Christ's death he expects his soul to be in company with Christ, at the nearest possible point to God, when he dies. But because Christ is to be the agent of the general resurrection, it is assumed that his body has risen too as the 'first fruits' of the general resurrection (1 Corinthians 15:20, 23). This is a deduction consequent upon the basic conviction that Jesus has been raised to God's right hand.

Thirdly, the deduction did not need to be tested because of the ambiguity of Jewish ideas of death and resurrection. The concept of resurrection/ascension (or of being 're-ceived up', Luke 9:51; cf. Mark 16:19; Acts 1:2, 11, 22; 1

Timothy 3:16; 'Gospel of Peter' 5:19) was pictured in terms of being awakened from sleep and rising out of the tomb and going up to heaven all in one act. Paul's deduction that Christ is the first fruits of the general resurrection is itself a rationalisation of this pictorial way of thinking. It is at this point that Matthew's incident of the 'bodies of the saints' (Matthew 27:51–53) is helpful, for it shows the persistence of this way of thinking in a Jewish–Christian milieu. It is most unlikely to have a historical basis, but it has symbolic value as one of the portents, like the earthquake and the rending of the temple veil, which convey the momentous importance of the fact of Christ's death. Thus, the outcome of this death was thought of in terms of bodily resurrection from the tomb, because that was the way of picturing it, but that did not necessarily entail the conclusion that the body was no longer in the tomb. In these circumstances there would be no point in opening the tomb to see if the body was there or not.

The growth of the tradition

Further reflection and debate on the proclamation of the gospel of the Resurrection inevitably led to a rationalising tendency, because questions were raised which had to be answered. I have suggested that Paul's idea of the first fruits is an example of such rationalisation.

In an entirely different setting the rising biographical interest in Jesus, which lies behind the formation of the written Gospels, was bound to evoke the demand for more detail about the fact 'that he was buried, and that he was raised on the third day' (1 Corinthians 15:4), which formed part of the basic proclamation. The story in Mark 15:42–16:8 (excluding 16:7) arose in response to this need. It gives the details of the burial, and extends that to include a portentous happening on the third day. There may be a historical kernel to the story, particularly in the association of Joseph of Arimathea with the tomb, but the details depend on knowledge of Jewish customs. The burial has to be hastened because of the beginning of the sabbath, and so the anointing of the body by the women must wait for the benefit of morning light on the third day at dawn. The fact that the stone has been rolled away and the tomb is empty corresponds with the way in which resurrection was pictured, as just explained, and objectifies it. The 'young man' within is a messenger (angel) to announce the gospel of the Resurrection. The silence of the women after such a terrifying disclosure explains why the story was so late in achieving circulation, and why it was unknown to Paul when he wrote to the Corinthians. It is this final detail, altered for obvious reasons by both Matthew and Luke, and by John in his story of Mary Magdalene, which gives away the comparative lateness of the tradition.

It is now generally agreed among scholars that Mark finished his Gospel at 16:8, verses 9–16 being a spurious addition which shows knowledge of Luke and possibly John. The idea that these verses replace an original ending of Mark which was subsequently lost is largely abandoned today. It is also clear that Mark knew that the earliest appearances of Jesus took place in Galilee (14:28, 16:7). We can conclude from these facts that he did not regard description of the appearances as part of his task of writing the life of Jesus. The Gospel of Mark carries numerous hints of the Resurrection (for example, the predictions in Mark 8:31, 9:31, 10:34), but preserves the sense that the Resurrection is a theological statement about Jesus rather than an item in his life story. Moreover, the fact that the empty tomb story does not include an appearance of Jesus shows that this was true also of the underlying tradition.

Once this story became current, it was inevitable that the focus of interest in the Resurrection as an event should shift from Galilee to Jerusalem, backed up by the memory that the Church's headquarters had been in Jerusalem until the outbreak of the Jewish War in AD 66. Matthew, Luke and John all have appearances of Jesus in Jerusalem on the third day, including the appearance to 'the twelve' (1 Corinthians 15:5), but corrected to 'the eleven' in Matthew 28:16; Mark 16:14; Luke 24:33. Matthew, however, retains the original tradition that this took place in Galilee (Matthew 28:16).

Further elaborations of the empty tomb story are the appearance to the women in Matthew 28:9–10, which may have derived from a variant of the same tradition in which Jesus replaces the angel; the dramatic presentation of this tradition as an appearance to Mary Magdalene alone in John 20:11–18; and the visit of Peter to the tomb in Luke 24:12, which also has a dramatic version involving another disciple in John 20:3–10. The fact that the foundation appearance to Peter himself (1 Corinthians 15:4; Luke 24:34) is nowhere described suggests that the development of the traditions was not primarily concerned with proof of the Resurrection but with its meaning in experience. This explains the meal-setting in the walk to Emmaus (Luke 24:30–35) and assembly of the Apostles (Luke 24:36–43; possibly also John 20:19–29, as it appears to reflect the Sunday Eucharist; see also John 21:9–14). For it was pre-eminently in the Eucharistic assembly that the presence of the Risen Jesus was experienced in the life of the Church.

At a later stage it seems that the empty tomb story was used apologetically in Jewish–Christian circles to rebut Jewish objections to the Christian claim that Jesus is the risen and glorified Son of God. It is assumed on both sides that the story is intended to give historical facts. By this time the empty tomb story could not be refuted because of the disruption caused by the destruction of Jerusalem. So the answer was to accuse the Christians of stealing the body of Jesus and making up the story of his Resurrection (see Matthew 28:13–15; Justin, 'Dialogue' 108). Matthew's account of the guards (Matthew 27:62–66, 28:11–15) is the Christian response. It makes the guards themselves witnesses of the arrival of the angel and the opening of the tomb. It probably accurately reflects current Jewish and Christian hostility in his day. It should also be noted that the tendency to incorporate resurrection predictions in the Jesus tradition is presupposed (Matthew 27:63). The story has been enormously expanded with further legendary details in the early second-century Gospel of Peter 8:28–11:49, which has a strongly anti-Judaic bias.

Luke and John represent very different tendencies from

Matthew. Luke rationalises the traditions by taking them factually, but presenting them reasonably with a considerable power of historical imagination which enhances their credibility. Luke is the only New Testament writer to suggest a limited period for the Resurrection appearances with a formal ending on Ascension Day (Acts 1:1–11), thus laying the foundation for the eventual pattern of liturgical celebration in the Church. John, on the other hand, builds up the dramatic possibilities inherent in the traditions with the object of passing beyond a factual understanding of them to the achievement of personal Resurrection faith.

The contribution of Paul

Though Paul does not have any of these stories at his disposal, he rationalised the Resurrection traditions in his efforts to persuade some of the Corinthian converts to accept the notion of personal resurrection. The value of his contribution is that it represents constructive thought on the Resurrection without the influence of the popular stories. His basic ideas agree with known tendencies of Jewish thought, as we have seen. He accepts the primitive statement of the Resurrection, and shares the evidence for it in the list of appearances, even to the extent of adding his own experience to the list. He thinks of Jesus as the Risen Messiah exalted to God's right hand and reserved in heaven to be God's agent in the general resurrection and the judgement, which he expects imminently. Thus he expects to be still alive at the time of the Parousia (1 Thessalonians 4:17; 1 Corinthians 15:52, cf. 7:29–31). However, in the course of explaining this to the Corinthians he makes two points of great value.

First, he acknowledges that the body, which can be seen to decompose in the grave, cannot literally be reconstituted at the general resurrection. Instead he suggests a transformation, the putting on of an immortal and incorruptible body appropriate to eternal life (1 Corinthians 15:51–57). This is explicitly said to take place at the Parousia, when 'the trumpet will sound, and the dead will be raised imperishable,

133

and we shall be changed' (15:52). As he has argued all along that the bodily resurrection of Jesus is not in principle different from our own, we must conclude that he thinks of the Resurrection body of Jesus in similar terms. Thus he can accept the bodily resurrection of Jesus, and call him the first fruits, without bothering whether Jesus' mortal and corruptible body remained in the tomb. The question whether the tomb was empty is simply irrelevant.

Secondly, as the transformation which awaits us is to take the form of conformity to Jesus, changing 'our lowly body to be like his glorious body' (Philippians 3:21), it can be asserted that the transformation is already at work in us now through the action of the Holy Spirit (see Romans 8:9–17). It is a process, beginning now and continuing in the time of waiting after death and reaching its full measure at the Parousia. This concept gives point to his final exhortation to the Corinthians to 'be steadfast, immovable, always abounding in the work of the Lord, knowing that in the Lord your labour is not in vain' (1 Corinthians 15:58).

Here we see the most satisfactory interpretation not only of the bodily resurrection of Jesus himself but also of our own destiny. Thus the feeling that so many people have that the empty tomb is essential for Resurrection faith proves to be both unnecessary and misleading. It promotes reliance on unprovable historical details, and misses the burst of understanding of the meaning of God's act in Christ which is so briefly indicated in the list of appearances and demonstrated in the extra appearance (1 Corinthians 15:8), the conversion of Paul.

Notes

1. Luke 24:12 is omitted, or placed in the margin, in some modern translations, because it is missing from some important manuscripts. Recent work on textual criticism, however, has convinced many scholars that it should be accepted as part of the true text of Luke, and indeed it seems to be required by Luke 24:24.
2. Mark ends at 16:8 in the best manuscripts, and the longer ending, verses 9–20, and a shorter ending, found either before the longer one or

alone instead of it, are manifestly not in Mark's style, though added in many manuscripts.

3. All the references in this paragraph are available in English in Charlesworth (1983, 1985). The reference to 'The Apocalypse of Moses' will be found as Text B of 'The Life of Adam and Eve'.

Further reading

Alsop, J.E., *The Post-Resurrection Appearance Stories of the Gospel Tradition* (Stuttgart, London, 1975)

Charlesworth, J.H., (ed.), *The Old Testament Pseudepigrapha* (2 vols; London: Darton, Longman & Todd, 1983–5)

Fuller, R.H., *The Formation of the Resurrection Narratives* (London: SPCK; New York: Macmillan, 1971)

Hendrickx, H., *The Resurrection Narratives of the Synoptic Gospels* (rev. ed.; London: Geoffrey Chapman, 1984)

Lindars, B., 'Jesus Risen: bodily resurrection but no empty tomb', *Theology* 89, 1986, pp. 90–6

Marxsen, W., *The Resurrection of Jesus of Nazareth* (London: SCM, 1968)

O'Collins, G., *Jesus Risen: the Resurrection – what actually happened and what does it mean?* (London: Darton, Longman & Todd, 1987)

Perrin, N., *The Resurrection Narratives: A New Approach* (London: SCM, 1971)

Selby, P., *Look for the Living* (London: SCM, 1976)

Wilckens, U., *Resurrection* (Edinburgh, 1977)

8. God Who Raises the Dead: The Resurrection of Jesus and Early Christian Faith in God*

Richard Bauckham

The hope of resurrection is radical faith in God the Creator. In Judaism it was the necessary consequence of faith in the God of Israel. It was integral to Jesus' radical faith in God his Father. The same God defined himself for early Christianity as the God who raised Jesus from the dead. This close connection between biblical faith in God, the Resurrection of Jesus and the hope of resurrection for all is the theme of this chapter.

The God who makes the dead live

In Romans 4:17 Paul characterises Abraham's faith by describing the God in whom he believed as the God 'who makes the dead live and calls that which is not into being'. Faith is possible because God is that creative power who can be absolutely trusted. Everything that exists depends on him for its very existence. To trust in him is not to rely on the immanent possibilities of created life, but on the transcendent possibilities of the Creator. Even when all immanent possibilities of life run out – in death – he who is the source of all life can create new possibilities of life – in resurrection.

Thus belief in resurrection is very closely connected with an understanding of God. It is faith in 'the God who makes the dead live'. This description, which comes close to being a definition of God, was borrowed by Paul from Jewish lit-

* © Richard Bauckham 1993

urgical language (whence it is echoed again in 2 Corinthians 1:9 and John 5:21). The identical Greek words occur in the Egyptian Jewish writing (from the first century BC or the first century AD) Joseph and Aseneth, in which Aseneth's family 'gave glory to the God who makes the dead live' (20:7). This virtually amounts to saying that they pronounced the benediction which later formed the second of the Eighteen Benedictions: 'Blessed art thou, Lord, who makest the dead alive.' Paul's Greek in Romans 4:17 translates literally the Hebrew of this benediction (whereas in 2 Corinthians 1:9 he varies the language: 'the God who raises the dead'). The Eighteen Benedictions, later to become the chief prayer of Judaism, probably did not yet exist as a set of eighteen in Paul's time, but Paul's language is itself evidence of what is in any case likely: that many of the benedictions were already in common use before their later formulation as a set of eighteen.

Resurrection has a remarkable prominence in the Eighteen Benedictions. The benedictions give praise to God in the first three benedictions, before turning to petition in the fourth and following benedictions. In the first three God is praised as, respectively, the 'shield of Abraham' (that is, the God of the covenant with Abraham and his descendants), the God 'who makest the dead alive', and the 'holy God'. It is true that in Paul's time not all Jews believed in the resurrection of the dead and not all who did gave it the importance which it acquired in the Eighteen Benedictions. But the Eighteen Benedictions, in the centrality they assign to belief in resurrection for Jewish faith in God, do represent the direction in which much Jewish religion was moving at the time of Jesus and Paul. Early Christian faith, which of course in Paul's time belonged still within the ambit of Judaism, was in continuity with this direction.

In Romans 4:17 Paul appropriately reproduces the exact language of the well-known benediction, because he is describing Abraham's faith. His whole argument is to the effect that Christians, including Gentile Christians, share this faith of Abraham (4:16), but when he goes on to describe Christian faith as such in verse 24 he gives a significantly

137

Christianised form of the Jewish formula: we 'believe in him who raised from the dead Jesus our Lord' (cf. Romans 8:11; 1 Corinthians 6:14; 2 Corinthians 4:14). This certainly does not mean that the Jewish formula becomes obsolete for Christians. Describing his own experience of coming close to death and experiencing deliverance from death, Paul uses the Jewish formula on his own account: it happened 'so that we should rely not on ourselves but on the God who raises the dead' (2 Corinthians 1:9). But Paul's use of both formulas raises the question of the relation between them for Christian faith in God. Most of the first Christians, like Paul, already believed in 'the God who makes the dead live' before they believed that he had raised the crucified Jesus from the dead. What difference did the Resurrection of Jesus make to their faith in this God?

Before asking this question, however, two other questions must claim our attention. We must ask how far the characterisation of God as 'the God who makes the dead live' can be regarded as integral to the faith of Israel and to the faith of Jesus. Belief in resurrection was a late development of Israelite religion, which is evidenced, according to most scholars, in only a very small number of Old Testament texts (some think only in Daniel 12:2; many, probably most, scholars would add Isaiah 26:19; Psalms 49:15, 73:24; other possibilities are more debatable). Can the centrality which belief in resurrection attained for both much of later Judaism and for Christianity therefore really claim continuity with faith in the God who revealed himself to Israel? Moreover, resurrection is far from prominent in the recorded teaching of Jesus. It would be generally agreed that Jesus did share this belief with many Jews of his time, but that it was of central importance for his understanding of God and faith in God is less obvious. Can the centrality of belief in resurrection – including Jesus's own Resurrection – for early Christian faith in God therefore really claim continuity with faith in God as practised and taught by Jesus? If, as we maintained at the outset, belief in resurrection is very closely connected with the understanding of God, both these questions are very important.

Resurrection and the God of Israel

The argument of this section will be that although belief in resurrection was a late development of Old Testament faith, it was also a necessary consequence of faith in the God of Israel. Of course, its emergence was due to particular historical circumstances: the development of religious beliefs is never a process of sheer logic in an intellectual vacuum. But with hindsight it is possible to see that Yahweh was already 'the God who makes the dead live' long before he was explicitly said to be.

For the Old Testament it is axiomatic that all life is God's gift. It comes from him and remains absolutely dependent on him. When he withdraws the breath of life, all creatures return to the dust from which they came (for example, Genesis 2:7; Isaiah 42:5; Psalm 104:29–30; Job 34:14–15). This sense of God as the source of life and the sovereign power over it is expressed in the claim that he 'kills and makes alive' (Deuteronomy 32:39; 1 Samuel 2:6; 2 Kings 5:7; cf. Wisdom 16:13; Tobit 13:2; 4 Maccabees 18:18–19):

> The LORD kills and makes alive;
> he brings down to Sheol and raises up (1 Samuel 2:6).

> See now that I, even I, am he,
> and there is no god beside me;
> I kill and I make alive;
> I wound and I heal;
> and there is none that can deliver out of my hand
>   (Deuteronomy 32:39).

It was almost certainly on these passages that the later Jewish description of God, which, as we have seen, Paul quotes, as the God 'who makes the dead live' was based (the verb 'makes alive' is the same). In their Old Testament contexts they scarcely refer to the resurrection of the dead. Rather they characterise God as the living God of unlimited power, who can save his people alive out of the most serious threats to life. Unlike the impotent idols, he is the God of sovereign power whom none can resist (Deuteronomy 32:39). In des-

139

perate situations he intervenes: to give bread to the starving, children to barren women, a helping hand to the crushed and destitute, just as he also strikes down the proud and the self-assured, demonstrating that life is his gift (1 Samuel 2:4–8). He freely disposes of life, he bestows it, withdraws it, grants it again. Though the question of new life for the dead had not yet arisen, it is clear that if it should arise this God could raise the dead.

In the Old Testament God's power over life is characteristically shown in situations where the immanent possibilities of life seem to have run out. In such situations it becomes existentially clear that life is given by God and so, even when it is virtually lost, can be given back by God. The psalmists, threatened by premature death, felt death to be a hostile power which already had them in its grip. They were as good as dead. In saving them from death, therefore, God could be said to have brought them back from Sheol (Psalms 30:3, 86:13; cf. Isaiah 38:10, 17; Jonah 2:6). Just such an experience was also Paul's, we remember, when he 'despaired of life itself' and learned to rely on 'the God who raises the dead' (2 Corinthians 1:8–9).

That Paul understood the continuity between such Old Testament faith and belief in actual resurrection is also clear from Romans 4:17–21. When he attributes to Abraham faith in the God 'who makes the dead live' Paul is referring to Abraham's faith in God's promise about his descendants. Abraham maintained this faith when it seemed impossible that he could have a son to inherit the promise, since Sarah was barren, and his own body, at the age of a hundred, 'was as good as dead' (verses 4:19; cf. Genesis 17:17, 18:11; Hebrews 11:11–12). In other words, Abraham relied on the God whose creative power can give life even where the immanent possibilities of life have run out. The writer to the Hebrews sees the same faith at work in Abraham's willingness to sacrifice Isaac: even should Isaac die, God could fulfil his promise. In Abraham's intention, Isaac was as good as dead, and he received him back from God as though risen from the dead (Hebrews 11:17–19). The idea (highlighted by later belief in resurrection) is by no means being simply read back into the Old Testament. Rather, the same pattern occurs again and again in the Old Testament: it is characteristic of Yahweh's action. Not only Isaac, but also Jacob, Joseph and Samuel are born to barren women (Genesis 25:21, 29:31, 30:22–23; 1 Samuel 1). Joseph, given up for dead, is restored to his father. The people of Israel, consigned to extinction by Pharaoh, owe their existence as the people of God to his deliverance of them from that fate. When their national existence is extinguished in the exile, Ezekiel envisages a new creative act of God which will bring the dead bones of the nation to life (Ezekiel 37:1–14). Jonah is saved from the belly of the great fish as though from the belly of Sheol. Daniel is delivered from the lion's den, and Shadrach, Meshach and Abednego from the fiery furnace. Not inappropriately, in one of the later additions to Daniel, they praise God who has 'rescued us from Hades and saved us from the hand of death' (Daniel 3:88 LXX, Θ).

The stories in Daniel are especially important because they indicate a point of transition to the hope of actual resurrection. Daniel and his friends were virtually martyrs, condemned to death for their faithfulness to the God of Israel and his laws. In the face of death they rely on the God who is able to deliver them from death (Daniel 3:28, 6:23). Their faith is that of the psalmists and, like the psalmists, they are snatched by God from the very jaws of death. But their stories were told for instruction and encouragement in an age when other Jews, similarly condemned to death for their faithfulness to God's laws, died as martyrs. Later chapters of Daniel refer to them (11:33, 35, 12:10) and the books of Maccabees tell the paradigmatic story of the martyrdom of the mother and her seven sons (2 Maccabees 7; 4 Maccabees). It is probably not the case, though this has often been thought, that Jewish belief in the resurrection of the dead originated at this time, in the persecution by Antiochus Epiphanes. There are clear traces of it in some earlier literature (Isaiah 26:19; 1 Enoch 22). But it certainly becomes clear and prominent in connection with these martyrs (Daniel 12:2–3; 2 Maccabees 7:9, 11, 22–23, 28–29). In circumstances of martyrdom, hope for the resurrection of

141

the dead was the necessary consequence of faith in the God who can deliver his faithful people from death.

For God to be trusted to raise the dead it was not, of course, sufficient to know that he was the source of all life and sovereign over it. He *could* raise the dead, but why should he? Again because he is the God in whom Israel had always believed. He is the righteous God who can be trusted to vindicate the righteous against their oppressors. He is the God of gracious love who will not abandon his people to death in which no relationship with God is possible. These essential elements of Israelite faith in God, which are so prominent in psalms which celebrate God's deliverance of the psalmist from threats of premature death, eventually pressed some of the psalmists in the direction of hope for final deliverance from death. It seems they were assisted in formulating this hope by the examples of Enoch and Elijah, the two men in the biblical story who as exceptional cases escaped death absolutely and were taken up into the presence of God. When two of the psalmists express the hope that God 'will receive' them (Psalms 49:15, 73:24), the verb (*lāqaḥ*, to receive, to take) is that used of God's translation of Enoch and Elijah to heaven (Genesis 5:24; 2 Kings 2:3). Both these psalms are preoccupied with the problem of the prosperity of the wicked. They discover hope in the reflection that the fate of those who trust in God must be different from that of those who trust in riches. This is not simply a question of retribution. It is rather that the person for whom knowing God is everything (Psalm 73:25–26) cannot believe that he will be deprived of this relationship (73:23–24). To know the living God is to know that one's life can be absolutely entrusted to him: 'My flesh and my heart may fail, but God is the strength of my heart and my portion forever' (73:26). In this faith nothing is new (cf. Psalms 11, 16, 23, 34; Lamentations 3:1–24) except that it now transcends death. The God whom believers had always trusted to deliver them from death is now trusted even to raise them from death.

These psalms make it clear that the hope of life with God beyond death did not originate only in connection with martyrdom. The Jewish hope of resurrection was never limited to the martyrs. But the martyrs remain paradigmatic for the hope of resurrection because the martyrs are those who so trust God with their lives that they can give them up for him. Two further themes of importance for early Christian faith can be mentioned in connection with this. The first is that in 2 Maccabees 7, the story of the martyrdom of the mother and her seven sons, hope of resurrection is possible because of faith in the Creator. God who brought all things into being out of nothing will 'give life and breath back' to the martyr after his death (vv. 11, 23, 28). The connection is the same as Paul makes in Romans 4:17 (God 'who makes the dead live and calls that which is not into being'), where the second clause, like the first, is a traditional liturgical one (cf. 2 Baruch 21:4, 48:8; Philo, *De Specialibus Legibus*, 4:187). The God whose word calls into being all that exists can recall into being all that has lapsed into non-being. Hope for new creation does not devalue creation or replace faith in the Creator. On the contrary, it arises out of radical faith in the Creator who can be trusted to remain faithful to his creation even beyond death.

Secondly, in the Maccabean period martyrdom was understood as sacrificial death on behalf of the nation (Testament of Moses 9; 2 Maccabees 7:37–38; 4 Maccabees 6:28–29, 17:21–22). This theology of martyrdom probably derived from Isaiah 53, where the Servant of the Lord, who suffers as a sacrifice for the sins of his people, is vindicated by God after his death (vv. 10–12; cf. Daniel 12:2). This theology of martyrdom, as we shall see, offered early Christians a way of understanding the exceptional nature of the Resurrection of Jesus.

Resurrection and the God of Jesus

Jesus preached and practised radical faith in the God of his people Israel. The God he called Father is the Creator of all life and the one who provides for all life (Matthew 7:26, 30, 10:29). He is recognised as Father when he is known as the one who made us, loves us, cares for us and can be

143

trusted. But in a world of sin, suffering and death, the
Creator and Provider is also the Redeemer and Renewer of
all life. To know him as Father is to trust the future to him,
to trust that in his faithfulness to his creation he will establish
the kingdom of his fatherly love. As the sovereign Source of
all life, the Father's will transcends the processes of sin,
suffering and death which ravage his creation and aims at a
renewal of creation which Jesus anticipates in his ministry.
Out of the transcendent future of God's kingdom Jesus
brings new possibilities of forgiveness, reconciliation, healing, provision of daily needs, victory over evil, peace with
the natural world. There is no sharp line in Jesus' thought
between creation and kingdom. The kingdom is at odds
with evil but not with creation. It surpasses the immanent
possibilities of creation, but at the same time renews and
fulfils them in its own transcendent possibilities. Radical
faith in the Creator is therefore also radical hope for his
kingdom.

One important strand of Jesus' teaching calls for radical
faith in God's care and provision for all needs. Since one's
life and all that sustains it come from the Creator, who knows
our needs and like a good father is only too ready to supply
them, God can be absolutely trusted with basic needs
(Matthew 6:8, 7:25–33, 7:7–11, 10:29–31). In faith it is possible to live without any security of one's own, dependent
from day to day on God's provision (Matthew 6:11, 34; Mark
6:8). This radical faith in God is connected with Jesus' radical demand for love. It is when life is seen and lived as
wholly given to one by God that one is freed from self-
possession and for self-giving. What has been freely received
can and must be freely given (Matthew 10:8). Radical faith
creates a reciprocal relationship between being given oneself
(by God) and giving oneself (in love). In the knowledge
that one owes everything to God the self-seeking drive to
secure one's own life and future at others' expense can
be abandoned. Indeed, one can recognise its futility (Luke
12:16–21; Matthew 6:19). Trusting oneself and one's future
to God who alone can be trusted with them, one is free to

144

risk oneself and give all that one has in love for others and
the service of his kingdom.

So Jesus' teaching about discipleship goes beyond trust
for daily provision to renunciation of possessions, self-denial
and self-sacrifice (Luke 14:26–33). Characteristically, Jesus
teaches that what is given up will be more than matched by
what is received from God (Mark 10:29–30). Treasure on
earth is exchanged for treasure in heaven (Mark 10:21;
Matthew 6:19–21). The parable of the talents (Matthew
25:14–30) makes the risk of financial investment a metaphor
for essentially the same point. Such teaching is not meant
to give a selfish motivation to the life of discipleship, as
though it were merely a more effective way of securing one's
own good for oneself. Rather, Jesus' teaching embodies the
paradox that only by denying oneself can one find self-
fulfilment. Only by abandoning the attempt to secure one's
own good and forgetting oneself in the service of God and
others can one's own true good be received – from God
(Mark 10:30) and from others (Luke 16:9). The paradox is
necessary for faith in the God who is faithful to his creation
and desires the good of all. The paradox can be lived only
through radical faith in this God. It is because one's own
future can be confidently entrusted to him that one can give
oneself to him in self-forgetting love for others.

Losing and saving one's life
In such teaching Jesus takes life beyond death for granted
(Matthew 6:20; Mark 10:30; Luke 16:9), but there is one
saying of Jesus which shows how integral was the hope of
resurrection to Jesus' understanding of living in radical faith.
This is one of the riddling aphorisms in which Jesus encapsu-
lated the central themes of his teaching: 'He who saves his
life will lose it, and he who loses his life will save it.' The
saying is unusually well attested. It occurs six times in the
Gospels, and these six occurrences probably reflect four
independent traditions. The four independent versions are
as follows:

(1) Whoever would save his life will lose it;

and whoever loses his life *for my sake and the Gospel's* will
save it (Mark 8:35)
(Matthew and Luke have parallels to this Marcan form of
the saying in Matthew 16:25 and Luke 9:24, but Matthew
16:25 is probably influenced by version 2 below.)

(2) He who finds his life will lose it;
and he who loses his life *for my sake* will find it (Matthew
10:39).

(3) Whoever seeks to gain his life will lose it;
and whoever loses his life will preserve it (Luke 17:33).

(4) He who loves his life (psychē) loses it;
and he who hates his life (psychē) *in this world* will keep
it *for eternal life* (zōē) (John 12:25).

The italicised words must be regarded as interpretative
additions, designed to make clear the meaning of the somewhat enigmatic saying. The additions 'for my sake' and 'for
the sake of the Gospel' (in versions 1 and 2) explain that the
kind of 'losing' of life which the second half of the saying
intends is not mere recklessness, but self-sacrifice out of
devotion to the cause of Christ. The additions 'in this world'
and 'for eternal life' (in version 4) are characteristically
Johannine phrases added by the Evangelist to make the
eschatological import of the saying explicit. These various
additions are by no means foreign to the meaning of the
saying, but they must be regarded as interpretations of a
saying whose originally simple and symmetrical form is preserved in version 3. The other differences between the versions are largely translation variants.

The word *psychē*, used in all versions of the saying for the
'life' that is lost or saved, strongly approaches the meaning
'self.' It reflects an Old Testament background of thought
in which the self is not easily separable from physical life,
but is concretely actualised in the life that one leads. The
provocative paradox of the saying challenges one to consider
what is *true* life or one's *real* self. But only in the context of

Jesus' call to radical faith does the challenge really make sense.

The first line has an obvious meaning. The attempt to secure one's life by living it for one's own benefit is bound to fail, because death comes to everyone and is the end of what the selfish person is trying to keep. To live one's life as though one owns it and can use it and keep it for oneself is to live an illusion which death will brutally destroy, as the rich fool discovered. That life is given by God and cannot be secured but only received from him emerges undeniably but too late when he takes it back in death. But there is also a sense in which living for oneself destroys life already before death. In grasping and hoarding his life for his own enjoyment, the selfish person finds the real fulfilment he seeks to achieve escapes him even before life itself escapes him in death. His true self cannot be found that way.

The person, on the other hand, who renounces the foolish attempt to keep his life for himself, who denies himself and lives for God and for others, finds his life given back to him by God. Before or after death? The various contexts in which the Evangelists placed the saying show that they certainly envisaged martyrdom as the extreme case of losing one's life, but some at least of these contexts (most unequivocally Luke 9:23–24) also require a broader application to the renunciation of self throughout a life of discipleship. Intriguingly, with whichever sense of losing life one starts, one finds it implies the other, too.

The person who expends his life in self-giving finds himself in this life of self-giving. He finds his true reality continuously given him by God as he gives himself for God. But then, for someone who so lives out of trust in God, it is inconceivable that the extreme act of self-giving, the death of a martyr, should fall outside the scope of the saying. If self-giving is the way to true life, then *a fortiori* martyrdom must be.

Alternatively, one can begin with martyrdom. The person who gives up his life in Christ's service entrusts his life to the power and the faithfulness of God. But if the receiving of one's true eternal self is through the giving of oneself, this must also be true of all self-giving short of martyrdom. In the self one receives anew from God at every stage of self-expenditure, one is already becoming the self one will receive at the resurrection. At every step on the way of the cross the life of the resurrection is anticipated, because giving oneself for God and receiving oneself from God are reciprocally related in radical faith. Thus it is not one life that one loses (mortal life in death) and another that one gains (eternal life in resurrection), but the same self that one is in self-giving one receives from God both now and eternally. 'Resurrection is the final actualisation of the fact that man receives his life wholly as a gift from the hands of God' (Schweizer).

The saying demonstrates that the hope of resurrection was not, for Jesus, merely an inherited belief which he assumed without reflection. He penetrated its roots in Jewish faith and found it an integral part of the radical faith he preached and practised.

The God who raised Jesus Christ from the dead

Jesus' words about losing and finding life were fulfilled in his own living, dying and Resurrection. The Synoptic Evangelists recognise this by placing the saying after the first Passion prediction and in immediate connection with Jesus' call to disciples to carry the cross after him (Matthew 16:21–25; Mark 8:31–35; Luke 9:22–24; cf. Matthew 10:38–39). John indicates even more emphatically that the saying is fulfilled primarily and paradigmatically in Jesus and only secondarily in disciples who follow him. He does so by placing it after a unique parabolic saying which has a good claim to be an authentic parable of Jesus: 'Truly, truly, I say to you, unless a grain of wheat falls into the earth and dies, it remains alone; but if it dies, it bears much fruit' (John 12:24).

The image is a traditional Jewish picture of resurrection: the seed, dead and buried in the earth, receives new life. The picture could be used to make various different points about resurrection (cf. Paul's use of it in 1 Corinthians 15:35–44). Jesus' distinctive use focuses on the point that

148

only through death can the seed *bear fruit,* that is to say, not only receive new life for itself but also *propagate* life. In thus adapting the image, Jesus applies it specifically to the death of a martyr who, according to Jewish martyr theology, benefited others through his death as a sacrifice for others. The earliest Christian interpretations of the cross understood Jesus, in the light of Jewish martyr theology, as the *eschatological* martyr, the one whose death *finally* achieved salvation *for all.* As his life and his death were his self-giving for all people, so his Resurrection is for us all. As Jesus received his life from God, never as a gift purely for himself but always as life to be given for others, so his risen life, received from God beyond the absolute self-giving of his death, is given to him for others. The Resurrection is God's gift of Jesus's risen self *to us.*

Risen with Christ

It is important at this point to recall that Jesus' Resurrection failed to conform to the Jewish hope of resurrection in one important respect: it occurred *before* the resurrection of all other people. The Jewish hope for resurrection was that all would rise at the end of this present age of history. This was because it arose in the context of the older hope for the arrival of God's kingdom, for the fulfilment of God's purposes for his people as a nation and for the world. Those who hoped for the achievement of God's righteousness in history would be raised to share in it. Thus, although there is some truth in the claim that the emergence of hope for resurrection witnesses to a greater sense of the distinct value of the individual, the hope was never purely individualistic (except perhaps in some rare cases where Hellenistic influence promoted this). It was a hope for the individual in community with others and in solidarity with the whole of God's creation. In such a context of thought, Jesus' Resurrection ahead of all others was not understood as a purely private experience, nor even merely as his vindication and legitimation by God as Messiah and Lord. He rose uniquely ahead of all others *because* he rose uniquely *for* all others.

149

The hope of resurrection was already actualised in his case as God's promise and gift of resurrection to the rest of us.

Precisely how the various New Testament writers relate Jesus' Resurrection to ours differs, but they show an impressive convergence in the belief that his Resurrection *entails* the resurrection of those who believe in him. Acts 3:15 calls Jesus 'the pioneer of life, whom God raised from the dead': he pioneered the way for others to follow. In Revelation 1:18 the Risen Christ declares himself, 'the living one; I died, and behold I am alive for evermore, and I have the keys of Death and Hades' – to release others from death. The Johannine Christ declares, 'I am the resurrection and the life; he who believes in me, though he die, yet shall he live, and whoever lives and believes in me shall never die' (John 11:25–26). Paul can say simply, 'he who raised Jesus will raise us also with Jesus' (2 Corinthians 4:14; cf. 1 Corinthians 6:14). He can express the point in terms of his Adam Christology: 'as by a man came death, by a man has come also the resurrection of the dead. For as in Adam all die, so in Christ shall all be made alive' (1 Corinthians 15:21–22). He can also put it in terms of his understanding of the divine Spirit as the Spirit of the Risen Christ: 'If the Spirit of him who raised Jesus from the dead dwells in you, he who raised Christ Jesus from the dead will give life to your mortal bodies also through his Spirit which dwells in you' (Romans 8:11).

The common thought is that God gives us our resurrection in Jesus' Resurrection. A further common thought follows from this: that in raising Jesus God has given him his own life-giving power to make the dead live. Hence, in Revelation 1:18 the Risen Christ bears the distinctively divine title 'the living one' (cf. Deuteronomy 5:26; Joshua 3:10; Psalms 42:2, 84:2; etc.); in 1 Corinthians 15:45 Christ as the eschatological Adam is 'life-giving spirit'; and most explicitly John 5:26 declares that 'as the Father has life in himself, so he has granted the Son to have life in himself' – so that he may give life (verse 21). These passages show how the New Testament's Christological understanding of resurrection is rooted in the fundamental Jewish understanding of God as the source of all life. Because the God who raises the dead has now raised Jesus from the dead, radical faith in that God is now Christological faith, focused on the Risen Christ. God's power to give life to the dead is the power of Jesus' risen life. Christian hope of resurrection is faith in Jesus who now *is* the resurrection and the life (John 11:25).

This is one aspect of the way Jesus' message underwent a Christological translation into the early Church's message about Jesus. Jesus' preaching of the kingdom of God was translated Christologically into the early Church's preaching of Jesus as Messiah. Jesus' understanding of God as Father was translated Christologically into the early Church's preaching of Jesus' sonship to God and knowledge of God as the Father of Jesus. Similarly, Jesus' aphorism, 'he who loses his life will find it', was translated Christologically into the preaching of Jesus' death and Resurrection. In each case, the subject of Jesus' preaching had been actualised in Jesus' own person and destiny, so that it became available to Christian faith through Jesus and in union with Jesus.

This does not mean that the message of Jesus' aphorism is superseded: its preservation in four strands of the Gospel traditions shows that this was not the early Christian view. But the message has been actualised for us in Jesus himself. Not only his losing his life – in self-giving to death – has been actualised for us, but also his finding his life beyond death, in God's gift of the Risen Jesus to us. Thus the radical faith which Jesus preached and practised becomes possible for us through faith in Jesus. It is in faith in Jesus that we receive our true selves from God. In identification with his death we find the possibility of giving ourselves in life and death. And in believing in his Resurrection we are able to trust God with our own future beyond death. This is expressed in the synoptic forms of the saying by the interpretative addition 'for my sake'. Pauline theology puts it in this way: 'he died for all, that those who live might live no longer for themselves but for him who for their sake died and was raised' (2 Corinthians 5:15). More personally: 'whatever gain I had, I counted as loss for the sake of Christ ... that I may know him and the power of his Resurrection, and may share his sufferings, becoming like him in his death,

151

that if possible I may attain the resurrection from the dead'
(Philippians 3:7, 10–11).

Conclusions

1. The hope of resurrection is radical faith in God the
Creator, who is the Source of all life, sovereign over all life
and remains faithful to his creation in renewing life even
beyond death. It is faith in the Creator which does not
limit his power to the immanent possibilities of creation but
entrusts the future to his transcendent possibilities.

2. Christian faith looks for transcendence of death only
as the gift of the transcendent Creator. Here lies the real
difference between anthropological theories of the immortality of the soul and the biblical hope of resurrection. It is
not so much a question of whether anything of us survives
death (in early Judaism and early Christianity it was not
usually denied that something survives, but this was not
resurrection). Rather, it is the difference between knowing
oneself as able to survive death and knowing oneself as given
by God and so entrusting oneself to him even in death. This
does not reduce the hope of resurrection to subjectivity, but
means that the objectivity of the risen life is God's gift and
is knowable only as God's gift.

3. It follows that we need to be careful about justifying the
hope of resurrection as coherent with a general anthropological characteristic of transcending every limit in search
of self-fulfilment (Pannenberg). This can sound all too like
the self-aggrandising rejection of all limits which has characterised the modern western project of human domination.
The biblical hope of resurrection coheres not with self-transcendence as self-preservation and self-aggrandisement, but
with self-transcendence as self-surrender in faith and self-
giving in love. Human life can be seen to be naturally orien-
tated to resurrection only when it is seen as given by God
and to be lived as God's gift.

4. Resurrection is a fresh creative act of God in which he
proves faithful to his creation by raising it to new life in his
presence beyond the reach of death. But resurrection is

anticipated in every experience of finding life through losing it – life rescued from the jaws of death, hope raised out of despair, freedom experienced in the face of oppression, forgiveness found beyond the vicious spiral of guilt and retribution, love given improbably to the unlovable, one's true self received through self-denial and self-giving. All such possibilities of this moral life are given by the Creator, who thus sustains, redeems and renews his creation in the face of evil and death. When they are seen and received as such, resurrection is not at odds with the created order of things, but the Creator's final act of faithfulness to his creation, consistent with the way this life before death is experienced in faith as his gift.

5. Thus the Resurrection of Jesus appears an unacceptable breach of the created order only if creation is deistically left to its own immanent possibilities. Certainly, the Resurrection of Jesus is unique within history, but its uniqueness belongs to Jesus' unique role in God's saving purpose. As the one who lived and died for all of us, Jesus was given new, risen life before all others for all others. If we receive the Crucified and Risen Christ as God's gift to us, we find in him that love of God from which not even death can separate us.

6. As radical faith in the Creator, the hope of resurrection does not diminish but confirms the value of this created world. As radical faith in the Creator, it is not escape into other worldly fantasy or an opiate of the people. Rather it is that fundamental entrusting of oneself and one's future to God which frees one really to live this life and to give oneself in love. In the end it makes possible the acceptance of death, not fatalistically or masochistically, not suppressing or abandoning the human protest against death, but transcending the protest in an affirmation of life as God's gift even in death.

Further reading

Benoît, P. and Murphy, R. (eds), *Immortality and Resurrection* (*Concilium* 10/6) (London: Burns & Oates, 1970)

Dautzenberg, Gerhard, *Sein Leben Bewahren:* Ψυχή *in den Herrenworte der*

Evangelien (Studien zur Alten und Neuen Testament 14) (Munich: Kösel, 1966)

Dodd, C.H., *Historical Tradition in the Fourth Gospel* (Cambridge: Cambridge University Press, 1963), pp. 338–43, 366–9

Hasel, G.F., 'Resurrection in the Theology of Old Testament Apocalyptic', *Zeitschrift für die alttestamentliche Wissenchaft*, 92 (1980), 267–84

Hofius, O., 'Eine altjüdische Parallele zu Röm. IV. 17*b*', *New Testament Studies*, 18 (1971–72), 93–4

Martin-Achard, R., *From Death to Life: A Study of the Development of the Doctrine of the Resurrection in the Old Testament* (Edinburgh/London: Oliver & Boyd, 1960)

Moltmann, J., *God in Creation* (London: SCM, 1985), pp. 268–70

Nickelsburg, G.W.E., *Resurrection, Immortality, and Eternal Life in Intertestamental Judaism* (Harvard Theological Studies 26) (Cambridge, Mass.: Harvard University Press, 1972)

O'Collins, G., *Jesus Risen* (London: Darton, Longman & Todd, 1987)

Pannenberg, W., *Jesus: God and Man* (London: SCM, 1968), pp. 74–88

Perkins, P., *Resurrection: New Testament Witness and Contemporary Reflection* (London: Geoffrey Chapman, 1984)

Schürer, E., *The History of the Jewish People in the Age of Jesus Christ (175 BC–AD 135)*, revised by G. Vermes, F. Millar and M. Black, II (Edinburgh: T. & T. Clark, 1979), pp. 455–63

Schweizer, E., 'ψυχή D. The New Testament', *TDNT* IX, pp. 637–56

Stemberger, G., *Der Leib der Auferstehung* (Analecta Biblica 36) (Rome: Biblical Institute Press, 1972)

Strawson, W., *Jesus and the Future Life: A Study in the Synoptic Gospels* (London: Epworth, 1959)

van der Walle, A., *From Darkness to the Dawn* (London: SCM, 1984)

154

9. The Resurrection and the Incarnation*

Brian Hebblethwaite

Introduction

Peter Carnley begins his magisterial study *The Structure of Resurrection Belief*[1] by noting how little space was given to discussion of the Resurrection in the book *The Myth of God Incarnate*. But the Incarnation, he argues, cannot be considered apart from its relation to the Resurrection. Indeed, Resurrection belief was prior to Incarnation belief, the latter depending on the former. Resurrection belief, he suggests further, has not only a temporal but also a logical priority over belief in the Incarnation.

In this essay I intend to examine the relation between the two beliefs, the two doctrines, and the two events (if, indeed, events they were). Clearly, it is important to distinguish the question of the relation between *belief* in the Resurrection and *belief* in the Incarnation from the question of the relation between the Resurrection and the Incarnation themselves. The dependence relation may be quite different between the two *events* from what it is between the two *beliefs*. Priority in the order of being may indeed be quite the reverse from priority in the order of knowing.

Four topics will be dealt with here. I consider first the Resurrection as *evidence* for the Incarnation. This section will be concerned primarily with belief, with the question whether it was the Resurrection of Jesus that led to belief that he was God incarnate. Secondly, I consider the Resurrection and the *meaning* of the Incarnation. Here we are

* © Brian Hebblethwaite 1993

primarily in the realm of doctrine, where the question concerns the interdependence of the doctrine of Christ's Resurrection and the doctrine of the Incarnation. This will necessarily require reflection on the theme of eschatology. What do both the Incarnation and the Resurrection mean for the future of creation? A related topic will be considered in the third section, namely the Resurrection and the *uniqueness* of the Incarnation. I shall argue that the theological incoherence of the notion of multiple incarnations follows, in part at least, from what Christians hold to be the case regarding the Risen Christ through all eternity. Finally, I come back to earth and, in the fourth section, consider briefly the bearing of both Incarnation and Resurrection on the Christian *moral life*, in both its personal and social dimensions.

The Resurrection as evidence for the Incarnation

It has frequently been suggested that it was the Resurrection of Jesus from the dead that opened the eyes of the disciples to his divinity. The instinctive reaction to the appearances of the Risen Christ was the response of worship. Doubting Thomas, confronted by the Risen Christ, cries out, 'My Lord and my God',[2] and only in the light of the Resurrection and of the early Christians' continuing encounter with the Risen Christ in prayer and Eucharistic worship did the process of reflection on who Christ was culminate in the conviction that he was the incarnate Son of God. The disciples may already, prior to his death, have discerned in Jesus the hoped-for Messiah, the Christ of God; but that conviction fell far short of belief in his divinity. Incarnational belief cannot plausibly be attributed to the disciples prior to the first Easter, and even then it was no more than embryonic. The Messianic hope had, in any case, been drastically transformed by the Crucifixion. It was the Resurrection that both opened up the way to an understanding of the soteriological significance of a Crucified Messiah and made possible and necessary the high Christology of the Johannine prologue and eventually the Chalcedonian definition.

But why, it may be asked, should the Resurrection be held to constitute sufficient evidence for belief in Christ's divinity? By itself, the claim that X has risen or been raised from the dead does not necessarily imply divinity. No one attributed divinity to Lazarus, for example. And none of us who hope one day to be raised to the life eternal expect thereby to be revealed as having been divine. (The sense, if any, in which our destiny – being raised with Christ – is to be described as 'divinisation' is quite different from what is meant by speaking of Jesus Christ as God incarnate.) So neither resurrection in the sense of restoration to one's previous animated bodily state, as in the case of Lazarus, nor resurrection in the sense of transformation into the 'spiritual Body' of the world to come, by itself entails divinity.

The Resurrection of Jesus is clearly closer to the latter than to the former case. The Risen Christ was certainly not a reanimated corpse. Jesus' Resurrection has indeed been held to constitute the anticipation of the final transformation of all God's personal creatures into the glorified state of heaven. But even as such it does not prove divinity. It is a notable thing that a Jewish scholar, Pinchas Lapide, can be disposed to accept the Resurrection of Jesus, without, of course, inferring his divinity.[3]

So what was it about *this* Resurrection that made and makes Christians respond with worship and discern in Jesus Christ alone God's incarnate Son? I note six atypical features in the case of Jesus' Resurrection that might be held, together, to account for this unique response.

In the first place, we have to consider the very special *characteristics* of the one now held to have been raised. He was, after all, the one whose authoritative teaching and mighty works had already invited interpretation in Messianic categories. I have already conceded that Messianic categories would not themselves have entailed divinity, but, all the same, Jesus' confident claim to speak and act as God's own representative had already set him apart from any other. The disciples, we read, had believed that it was he who was to redeem Israel.[4]

Then, secondly, we have the *appearances* of the Risen Christ

157

to the disciples, as listed by St Paul in 1 Corinthians 15 and described, no doubt with some embellishments, at the end of Matthew, Luke and John and in the addition to Mark. More than anything else, it was these appearances that transformed the disillusioned disciples into preachers of a new age. In no other case do we hear of comparable phenomena. Admittedly, the nature of the appearances is hard to determine. But they cannot possibly be regarded as stories of encounters with a reanimated corpse. Nor does the nineteenth-century 'subjective vision' hypothesis retain much psychological credibility. The Easter narratives, rather, are uniquely suggestive of some objective manifestation from beyond the natural sphere.

Similarly, and in the third place, we cannot ignore the stories of the *empty tomb*. It might be thought that, having dismissed the view that the Resurrection of Jesus was a matter of the reanimation of a corpse, we could view lightly the empty tomb tradition and treat it, without qualms, as a later legend. Just as we no longer believe that *our* eventual resurrection – our transformation into the new creation of heavenly glory – will involve the emergence and reassembly of our flesh and bones from the grave (or crematorium), so we need no longer think of Jesus' Resurrection as requiring an empty tomb.[5] Certainly, there are some resurrection narratives in the Gospels – the 'saints' emerging from their tombs (Matthew 27:53) and the Risen Jesus eating fish (John 21:9–14) – which we do have to regard as legendary, if we are serious about distancing ourselves from the 'resuscitated corpse' conception of the Resurrection. But the empty tomb is rather different. The arguments in favour of this element in the tradition are strong, even if they fall short of proof: the inability of the opponents of the Christians to produce the body, the absence of any evidence of the story having been disputed at the time, the primary role of *women* as witnesses to the empty tomb (a detail no one would invent in a culture which despised the testimony of women). Moreover, even if it was not *necessary* for the tomb to have been empty for resurrection in the sense of change into the glorified mode of heavenly existence, it may have been a necessary *sign*, not only of that transformation, but of its unique significance in the whole story of God's dealings with the human race. Furthermore, the empty tomb provides a specific and *historical* basis for belief in the Resurrection, though the Resurrection itself quite clearly transcends the historical.

Fourthly, we may underline the fact, stressed by David Brown in his account of these matters in his book *The Divine Trinity*, that it was conviction of the *exalted status* of the Risen Christ, not simply the fact of his Resurrection, that evoked the response of worship and the assertion of his unique significance.[6] We may be unable to pinpoint precisely what it was that led the Gospel writers to put into the mouth of the Risen Christ the words, 'all authority in heaven and in earth has been given unto me',[7] but clearly we have a basis here for the growing supposition that Jesus Christ had not only spoken with God's authority but had come to them himself from the side of God.

The same may be said, fifthly, in respect of the universal *soteriological efficacy* of the Christ event which finds expression as early as the letters of St Paul. That the Risen Christ was both experienced and interpreted as Saviour, and uniquely so, is quite clear from the way the New Testament authors write of his significance. We do not have to press back behind the interpretations that we find in Paul, the author of the letter to the Hebrews, and John to some identifiable pure experience in order to appreciate the soteriological factors that led to the conviction of Christ's divinity. The Risen Christ was 'experienced as' Saviour, and God alone could save.[8]

In the sixth place, and bound up with all the aforementioned features, we have to reckon with the undoubted fact that the early Christians believed themselves to exist in relation to the Risen Christ as a living Lord. Whether in prayer or in sacrament or in fellowship, they experienced his presence as a mutual *indwelling*, they in him and he in them. It was Paul, again, who articulated this in terms both of being 'in Christ' and of Christ's Spirit being in him and his fellow Christians.[9] This too is a unique phenomenon. Of

159

no other human being is it claimed that an ever-present spiritual and sacramental relation is both possible and real.

It is reasonable to hold that all these factors – the authority of Jesus of Nazareth himself in speaking and acting for God, his resurrection from the dead, vouched for by a series of appearances and by the empty tomb, the enhanced authority of the risen and exalted Lord, his experienced soteriological efficacy and his living presence in the worship and life of the Christian communities themselves – all these factors together contributed to the growing conviction of Christ's divinity and eventually to the doctrine of the Incarnation.

We may well ask to what extent, in appealing to the Resurrection, with this whole context in mind, as evidence for the Incarnation, we are appealing to historical evidence as such. Well, Jesus and the impression his life and teaching made, the records of his appearances, the empty tomb, the swift emergence of 'high' Christologies in connection with belief in his exaltation, in his saving power, and in his living presence in the worshipping communities of Christians, are all historical facts, to be sifted and weighed by students of the New Testament. Equally clearly, the Resurrection itself, Christ's sacramental presence, and his saving power, are trans-historical realities, if indeed realities they are. Moreover, the last two factors mentioned here are trans-historical realities in which subsequent generations of Christians, including ourselves, have claimed and claim to share. It may well be thought that participation in these mysteries opens the eyes of Christians to the real significance of the historical factors to which we appeal in justification of our faith. This apparently circular argument is hardly a vicious one, however; for the purely historical evidence poses questions and suggests hypotheses which participation can and does then verify.

The Resurrection and the meaning of the Incarnation

It has been said by Wolfhart Pannenberg that the Resurrection retroactively constitutes the divinity of Christ.[10] It is hard to see what this could possibly mean. The conclusion to

160

which several of the New Testament writers and most of the Church Fathers eventually came, in the light of the factors mentioned in the previous section, was that Jesus of Nazareth was divine all along – that he was, as the later terminology put it, God the Son incarnate, all along. Admittedly, he would not have been understood in these terms had he not been raised from the dead. But the Resurrection cannot meaningfully be thought of as having had retrospective *ontological* force. Resurrection *belief* may have logical as well as temporal priority over Incarnation belief, but not the Resurrection over the Incarnation.

It might still be asked, however, whether it makes sense to say that Jesus might have *been* God incarnate even if he had not been raised from the dead. The supposition makes little or no sense in Christian terms. It is Church doctrine that God in the Person of his Son took humanity into himself for all eternity, and that entails resurrection. It does not, however, entail the manifestation of the Risen Lord within the structures of this formative stage of the creative process, to which the appearances and the empty tomb bear witness. The point of the Incarnation, as far as we are concerned, no doubt requires such an anticipated manifestation this side of the grave. But we could imagine an incarnation and resurrection which only became apparent to us after death. So we have to be careful in specifying the sense in which incarnation *requires* resurrection.

Given Resurrection, not only in the sense of the raising of Christ to glory, but also in that of his anticipated manifestation this side of the gap between history and the eschaton, we can, of course, affirm the Incarnation as consisting in the whole life of Jesus – his earthly life from conception to his death on the Cross, and also his eternal glorified life in heaven. Taken together, Incarnation and Resurrection constitute the special way in which, according to the Christian religion, God interacts with his creation and binds it to himself for ever.

As we reflect on these mysteries in systematic theology, we realise that Incarnation and Resurrection must be taken together and that it was indeed a major fault of the dis-

161

cussions in *The Myth of God Incarnate* to have isolated the Incarnation for special scrutiny. Christians cannot hope to understand the Incarnation without reference to the Resurrection, for the latter not only brings out the permanent significance of the former but demonstrates the meaning of the Incarnation as the taking of humanity into God. The idea expressed in the less plausible versions of kenotic Christology that the earthly sojourn of the Son of God represented a temporary incarnation, the abandonment of divine prerogatives only to be followed by their resumption at the Resurrection, is a deeply incoherent theological idea. Resurrection cannot possibly mean the sloughing off of the human and the resumption of the divine. The divine is rather channelled through and manifested in the human both in the earthly life of Jesus and in his risen glorified humanity. This is one of the main differences between Christian incarnational belief and Hindu avatar belief.[11] Vishnu appears on earth in many temporary forms, animal and human, but the human form of Krishna, for example, is only a screen. In the great theophany of the *Bhagavadgita* the awesome deity himself is revealed behind the screen; and, of course, with the death of Krishna, Vishnu resumes his full unmediated deity.

According to Christian doctrine, by contrast, the infinite, interpersonal, mysterious God, while discernible abstractly to human reason and affectivity in the varieties of religious experience, is known concretely and personally only in so far as God renders himself thus knowable through Incarnation, Resurrection, and inspiration. But this is not just a question of our knowledge of God. The humanity of Christ is the vehicle of our union and communion with God through all eternity, as we who have been incorporated into Christ's risen body are raised into the life of heaven. In the communion of saints, in heaven as on earth, it is through Christ's glorified body that we continue to be embraced and sustained in the love of God. For the Incarnate and Risen Christ does not cease to be God's chosen mode of self-presentation to us and of our union with him. When we hope to see God in heaven, it is still God's human face, the risen and exalted

Lord, whom we hope to see. The abstractness and vagueness of human knowledge of God can only be overcome, even in eternity, by personal acquaintance with God's human face and by incorporation into God the Son's incarnate, risen, body. The Resurrection, therefore, is integral to the meaning of the Incarnation in the Christian scheme of things. It must be stressed again that this is a matter of ontology, not just of epistemology. Incarnation and Resurrection belong together in the order of being. For thus and only thus does God relate himself fully to us and us to him for ever. It is by taking our nature upon him in the Person of his Son that God accommodates his infinite mystery to our finitude and binds us to him in love. Incorporation into Christ's body, therefore, is the condition not only of our personal acquaintance with God but also of our God-given destiny in the consummation of all things. For the eschaton consists in nothing other than the perfect union of all finite personal centres with the eternal God–man in whom infinite and finite coinhere.

The Resurrection and the uniqueness of the Incarnation

It is these eschatological considerations that, especially, rule out, for Christian understanding, the idea of multiple incarnations. I have already indicated the difference between Christian incarnational belief and Hindu avatar belief, with its stories of many 'incarnations'. This is not a merely factual difference, with Christians as a matter of fact affirming a single incarnation, Hindus affirming many. It is a logical difference. For Christianity, the Incarnation is necessarily unique, and it is the Resurrection, whose significance for the Incarnation was spelled out in the previous section, that more than anything else requires and explains that uniqueness. It is not the only factor, of course. If God the Son were indeed to take our nature upon him and come among us as one of us, channelling his divine personality through a human personality that genuinely expressed not only his nature but himself, it could only be in and as a particular individual, once for all. The divine Son is not

163

a schizophrenic. His identity cannot be split among a series of human beings. But the Resurrection makes this necessary uniqueness even plainer. If humanity is taken into God for ever and the Risen Christ remains the focus of our relation to God through all eternity, then that eternal focus must be one. We do not, in the eschaton, expect to be encountered by a group of divine incarnations, themselves in theory capable of interpersonal relation. The manner in which the Risen Christ incorporates, inclusively, the whole of redeemed humanity is naturally not known to us now – though the way in which the whole Church on earth is held, already, to be the body of Christ and not the body of a series of 'Christs' is rightly seen as an anticipation of what we expect hereafter. As we shall see in the final section, our conformity to Christ, begun and in process here and now in our earthly lives and in the earthly city, is a matter of our relation to the one God–man in whom, in Bonhoeffer's words,[12] the ideal and the real are unified for all eternity. That process of conformation will be continued and perfected in the eschaton. It makes no sense to abandon the concept of God–man unity at that point and resort to an ultimate pluralism, even as a theoretical possibility. The Resurrection, therefore, underlines and confirms the necessary uniqueness of the Incarnation.

It may well be asked (quite speculatively, of course) whether these remarks are restricted in their scope to God's salvific and revelatory involvement with *humanity*. Jesus Christ may indeed be the incarnate, crucified and risen Son, raised to the right hand of God for all eternity, and the unique channel of communion with and conformation to the divine for all *human beings*. But what if there are other personal creatures on other planets in other galaxies, who equally need God's very self and essence all divine in *their* midst and in *their* form? Does it make sense to suppose that, without prejudice to the centrality of Jesus Christ as God made man for us and for our salvation, the same eternal Son or Word might take an extraterrestrial nature upon him and express his nature and personality in an 'incarnate' life for them? I think not. Such an 'incarnation' would also entail a 'resurrection' into eternity, by parity of reasoning with the human case. On this scenario, too, an ultimate pluralism in God would have to be affirmed – each form of life, human and extraterrestrial, being united to their Maker through incorporation into the risen 'body' of the appropriate mediator. But each mediator is, *ex hypothesi*, an incarnation of the same divine Word or Son. The same problem of attributing multiple incarnate personalities to the second Person of the Trinity would arise here as it did in the case of purported multiple human incarnations. Are *these* divine creaturely mediators held to be capable of communicating with each other in the eschaton? The supposition makes no theological sense, if they are all incarnations of one and the same divine Son. Similarly, it makes little sense to suppose that one and the same heaven consists in *different* sets of risen and glorified creatures, united with the same God in and through different divine creaturely 'bodies'. For each of these, ultimately speaking, would be one and the same inclusive personality. That makes no sense.

I suggest that it is only because the eschatological implications of incarnational belief have not been spelled out that philosophers of religion (and novelists) have been ready to toy with the idea of multiple incarnations – whether in the human or in some extraterrestrial context.[13]

Reflection on these issues leads us to hazard the speculation that humanity is indeed the unique form of creaturely personal existence, that God unites his personal creatures to himself uniquely through the Incarnation of his Son as man, and through Christ's unique and all-encompassing risen and glorified humanity, for all eternity.

It is fashionable to disparage such an anthropocentric world-view. But it must be pointed out that in fact anthropocentrism makes much the greatest theological sense in the light of the doctrines of Incarnation and Resurrection, taken together as constituting the heart of Christian understanding. A short sketch of such an anthropocentric Christian world-view will show how many other theological problems are resolved if God's creative plan is seen in the light of its Christ-centred consummation.

165

Let us suppose that it is logically impossible for God to create finite personal beings (angels, for example) directly, with no evolving physical cosmos to act as a screen between Creator and creature and as a quasi-independent basis for the formation of autonomous, self-reproducing creaturely persons. The whole physical universe is posited in being in such a way as to evolve, over time, the necessary conditions for the emergence of finite, rational, persons – their embodiment and their whole world being necessary aspects of their relative autonomy and of the values of finite personhood. (It may be pointed out here that we now have some evidence that the cosmos has to be as large as it is, and its rate of expansion and its early history have to be very much what they have been found to be, if ever life were to appear, even in one 'corner' of one galaxy. There are also scientific grounds for thinking that rational beings have not evolved elsewhere in the universe.[14]) Rootedness in a law-governed physical world, as well as making us possible, necessarily subjects us to the risks of suffering and evil. We are subject to accident and temptation.[15] In order to rescue us from this predicament and to effect our eternal destiny in the divine plan, God fashions, by his providence, a human context in which he can, without any crude manipulation, enter within the structures of his creation himself and live an incarnate life. By this means he at the same time takes the human predicament upon himself, sharing the risks of finite personhood to the point of dereliction, and also demonstrates in costly action, his love for all his personal creatures and his forgiveness of their wrongdoing. By then raising Christ from the dead and imparting his risen life to us – or, rather, by incorporating us into his risen life – he overcomes the limitations and negations inevitable in this formative phase of our creation, and re-creates us for eternity. God incarnate thus remains the channel and focus, not only of our redemption but of our eternal participation in the divine life. It is humanity and humanity alone (together with all the values of human life) that is taken into God, and so God has a *human* face for ever. There is no way of extending this vision to include different communities of other kinds of personal beings without forfeiting the special way in which God relates his creatures to himself – namely, by becoming, eternally, one of them. The one divine Son could not thus become two or more finite persons, human or otherwise. Conversely, from the facts of God's Incarnation in Jesus Christ and from his Resurrection we deduce that humanity is the only kind of finite personal being that there is. Anthropocentrism belongs as much to the Christian doctrine of God as to the Christian doctrine of creation.

Incarnation/Resurrection and the Christian life

In this final section I return to the earthly, formative, phase of God's creation of a world of finite centres of personal life and love, and ask what bearing the Christian doctrines of Incarnation and Resurrection have on the moral life of individuals and their societies here on earth.

Mention has already been made of the soteriological significance of both the Incarnation and the Resurrection. This must now be considered in ethical terms. For soteriology and ethics are inseparable. The overcoming of evil, the forgiveness of sins and reconciliation with God begin to take effect here and now in transformed lives and a more just social order, as Christians – and society – are progressively conformed to Christ by the Spirit of the Risen Christ. In the Christian tradition this process is named 'sanctification'.[16] Our present concern is with the way in which sanctification both follows the pattern of Incarnation and Resurrection and depends upon the Spirit of the Incarnate, Crucified and Risen Lord.

In his book *Resurrection and Moral Order*,[17] Oliver O'Donovan draws attention to the fact that specifically Christian ethics depend upon the Resurrection of Jesus Christ from the dead. And indeed it is in the power of the Resurrection that all things are made new. This is not just a matter of hope for the future beyond death. Incorporation into Christ and conformity to Christ begin here and now, and it is the Church's task to make known these possibilities and the actuality of the spiritual resources – the Spirit of the Risen

BRIAN HEBBLETHWAITE

Christ – given to us already for the transformation of life. O'Donovan also points to the foundation of Christian ethics in the Incarnation.[18] But he interprets this latter dependency more as a matter of the authority of Christ's teaching and life than in terms of the principle of incarnation which an older generation of Anglicans extracted from the story of God's own self-limitation in an incarnate life. There is scope for further reflection on the relation between both Incarnation and Resurrection and the moral life.

Certainly, the fact that God's way with his world of personal creatures is the way of self-involving love, as shown in the incarnate life of Christ, should inspire us to keep before our eyes the example of our Lord. The character of Christ is indeed the pattern and the norm of the Christian life. Any reference to the power of the risen and glorified Christ cannot be allowed to obscure the actual character of the love revealed to us in the life and teaching of the incarnate one. But the ethical significance of the Incarnation extends beyond the example and teaching of our Lord. The very pattern of Incarnation, like the way of the cross, transcends the centuries and yields an ethic of self-involvement, sacramental life and political commitment that in no way turns its back on material, earthly, realities. The Christian way is always that of transformation from within. The power of the Resurrection energises and enables precisely this way of overcoming evil. It does not negate it or relegate it to a preliminary stage. Certainly, the Resurrection guarantees that this way will in the end prevail, but it offers no short cuts. The active spiritual transforming power of the Risen Christ is the power of the one who humbled himself and trod the path to Calvary. That is our God and no other, and the promise of a perfected consummation in the end involves no bypassing of the need for discipleship here and now. Rather, it makes such discipleship possible and sustains it, come what may.

But equally it *is* the Resurrection of the incarnate one that confirms that this was indeed God's way with the world. It is the Resurrection that makes available the Spirit of the living Christ to draw us into the mystical body of the incarnate Lord. As O'Donovan rightly says, it is the Resurrection that makes all things new, and gives specifically Christian ethics its dynamism and transformative power. The Incarnation provides the content of Christian ethics, the Resurrection its capacity for realisation both here and in eternity.

This is as true of human social life as it is of individual sanctity. We are perhaps accustomed to think of the power of the risen life as manifesting itself in saintly lives like that of Mother Teresa of Calcutta, and so of course it does. But it equally manifests itself in the fellowship of Christians and in the promise of redeemed and transformed structures of communal life. As Joseph Fletcher observes, justice is love distributed,[19] and the power of the Resurrection is as much at work where justice comes to prevail as it is in the lives of those who love with something of God's love.

All the same, the power of the Resurrection does not abrogate the principle of incarnation in the social sphere. It is only by sacrifical self-involvement that structures, like lives, are Christianly transformed. So we may conclude that the Resurrection has no more priority over the Incarnation in ethics than it does in ontology. The content and the shape of the moral life, in both its personal and its social aspects, is given by the love of God incarnate. The Resurrection enables us to be drawn into that incarnate love. At the same time it assures us that such love will in the end be all in all.

Notes

1. P. Carnley, *The Structure of Resurrection Belief* (Oxford: Clarendon Press, 1987).
2. John 20:28.
3. P. Lapide, *Auferstehung: ein Jüdisches Glaubenserlebnis*, cited in Carnley, op. cit., p. 22.
4. Luke 24:21.
5. See the essay in this volume by Barnabas Lindars.
6. D. Brown, *The Divine Trinity* (London: Duckworth, 1985), ch. 3.
7. Matthew 38:18.
8. On the impropriety of the search for pure experience behind all interpretation, see N. Lash, *Easter in Ordinary* (London: SCM, 1988). On 'experiencing as', see J. Hick, *God and the Universe of Faiths* (Basingstoke: Macmillan 1973; London: Collins, Fount Paperback, 1977), ch. 3.

9. On the significance of Paul's 'in Christ' locutions, see C.F.D. Moule, *The Origin of Christology* (Cambridge: Cambridge University Press, 1977).

10. W. Pannenberg, *Jesus: God and Man* (Eng. trans.) (London: SCM, 1968).

11. See G. Parrinder, *Avatar and Incarnation* (London: Faber & Faber, 1970).

12. See D. Bonhoeffer, *Ethics* (Eng. trans.) (London: SCM, 1955; London: Collins, Fontana, 1964).

13. See T. Morris, *The Logic of God Incarnate* (Ithaca, NY: Cornell University Press, 1986), and C.S. Lewis, *Perelandra* (London: Bodley Head, 1943). Reprinted as *Voyage to Venus* (London: Pan, 1953).

14. See J.D. Barrow and F.J. Tipler, *The Anthropic Cosmological Principle* (Oxford: Clarendon Press, 1986).

15. See B.L. Hebblethwaite, 'The Problem of Evil', in G. Wainwright (ed.), *Keeping the Faith* (London: SPCK, 1989).

16. For the social significance of sanctification, see H. Berkhof, *Christian Faith* (Eng. trans.) (Grand Rapids, Mich.: Eerdmans, 1979).

17. O. O'Donovan, *Resurrection and Moral Order* (London: IVP, 1986).

18. Op. cit., pp. 143–7.

19. J. Fletcher, *Situation Ethics* (London: SCM, 1966), p. 87.

Further reading

Hebblethwaite, B., *The Incarnation: Collected Essays in Christology* (Cambridge: Cambridge University Press, 1987)

Lampe, G.W.H. and MacKinnon, D.M., *The Resurrection: A Dialogue between Two Cambridge Professors in a Secular Age* (London: A.R. Mowbray, 1966)

Torrance, T.E., *Space, Time and Incarnation* (Oxford: Oxford University Press, 1969)

Torrance, T.F., *Space, Time and Resurrection* (Edinburgh, Handsel Press, 1976)

10. Resurrection and Rationality*

Adrian Thatcher

This essay does not ask 'What happened at the Resurrection?' Instead, it asks what happened to the human capacity to accept, by rational means, the Resurrection as God's miraculous act. It suggests that the Resurrection is able to elicit a cognitive response from believers. The elements of this response are described, and the verdict reached that it is fully rational.

A satanic suggestion

Let us begin with a thought experiment. Descartes once imagined a malignant demon interfering with his thoughts. This time you are the demon. You decide you are going to undermine the belief of millions of people yet to be born in the Resurrection of Jesus Christ. In the course of doing this you will undermine much else besides. Your project is an audacious one. So you take a softly, softly approach. You take two or three centuries. You move imperceptibly. No one notices you at work.

You first encourage the human mind to separate the truths of reason from the truths of faith. You can then make one superior to the other. At the same time, you persuade people only to accept as knowledge those things of which they can be absolutely certain. You propose to use God's gift of science to further your purposes. You use the notion of 'natural laws' to make people think God is external to this

* © Adrian Thatcher 1993

world, available only by miraculous acts. Then you discredit miracles by saying the evidence is against them.

You make the human mind, operating within a strict empirical mould, the sole judge of what is to be believed in all matters, scientific, moral and religious. In this you have a problem. There are many Christians who believe that pride is a great sin, and that human fallenness extends to their rational powers. You cope with this by weakening the notion of sin generally, and providing other names for it. You want people to think that 'seeing is believing', so you allow the emerging sciences to emphasise the sense of sight above all others. Once you deceive people into identifying the real with the observable you surmise that religious faith in general will be defenceless against even mild empirical objections.

Your project is so important to you that you prepare additional measures, just in case the others should fail. You give people a new distinction (between facts and values) which you know they will like to use. In so doing you know they will insist on separating one from the other, and that will give a whole new slant to the question, 'But what really happened?' without anyone noticing that the rules of evidence have been changed. You will cause the notion of objectivity that scientists adopt to be so successful there will be room for no other version. Realism, then, will be whatever the scientists decide. To cap it all you persuade people to think of themselves as isolated individuals, separated both from the traditions that made them what they are and from each other. That way they will disregard altogether the wisdom of earlier generations (and take for granted that capitalism and competition are natural states). You persuade people alive now that they understand the world better than any of their predecessors. And just in case you begin to be rumbled, you arrange for philosophy departments to be weakened or closed down altogether (so that the historical causes of unbelief remain undetected and the foundations of all intellectual enquiry become weakened). Theology departments, which you have never had much cause to fear, you turn into religious studies information bureaux.

The climate of unbelief

Readers will not doubt that something very like this really has occurred. There is a 'climate of unbelief' (Thatcher, p. 439) in the western world the origins of which at last we are beginning to understand (Gunton; Newbigin; MacIntyre (1)). It has produced an 'epistemological impoverishment' which influences everyone, believers or not. Theology students have to grasp that, as contemporary citizens of a secularised country, they are heirs to a restricted rationality which has to be unlearned if the right questions are ever to be posed. The sociology of knowledge has, in the last twenty-five years, helped us to see that epistemic frameworks are bequeathed to us which are notorious in their capacities to mislead. Intellectual change, perhaps like social change, inevitably compels those caught up in it to look for continuities, and this in turn compels them to look again at the past.

The separation of reason and faith in the seventeenth century is well charted (Gunton; Kung). Unaided reason still permitted God to exist while the proofs of Descartes held. Once Hobbes and Hume tore them down, reason, now autonomous from the springs of faith, has been thought to lack a crucial ingredient, proof. Descartes's identification of knowledge with certainty (Meditation 1) brought into European thought impossible criteria by which to recognise real knowledge, and British empiricism from Locke to Wittgenstein has wrestled with the Cartesian problem ever since. The Newtonian world-view emptied the physical world of God's presence leaving either the soul (the inner world), or miracle (that is, violation of the laws of nature), as the *loci* of divine activity (Hume). We owe to Hartley the beginnings of the mechanisation of the soul, to Kant the necessity for religion within the limits of reason alone, to Bentham and Mill the reduction of morality to calculation. The triumph of scientific materialism in nineteenth-century Britain (Coley and Hall) leaves radical empiricism in control of our thoughts. To the Vienna Circle and to A.J. Ayer we owe the assumption that our beliefs must pass the stringent verifi-

173

cation test if they are ever to be accorded the status of knowledge.

This list is hopelessly inadequate even as a sketch: readers in search of more detail should consult MacIntyre. But no attempt is being made to describe the climate of unbelief; only to suggest that we hold our beliefs in such a climate, and that the roots of it are accessible to students of the history of ideas. I am more concerned with the effect that epistemological impoverishment has on our capacity to hold religious beliefs at all and on our ability to perceive the import of religious claims. In this respect belief in the Resurrection is a good test case for other religious beliefs. Can there be a broader, more religiously sensitive rationality? Before suggesting the elements of one, it is necessary to make some disclaimers.

Disclaimers

First, there is no mileage for Christian theology down the road of fideism, that is, the view that faith does not require rational justification. Once severed from its rational basis, Christian faith is powerless to distinguish itself from fanatics, freaks and fundamentalists. Hume and Wittgenstein warn us that the stranger our story the more likely it is that some people will believe it. A parallel cul-de-sac leads to a special, religious rationality with its own rules and procedures. Only the *illuminati* know what's what. On the other hand, a rationality which is blatantly unsympathetic to religious claims must be resisted in the name of reason as well as faith. Christians must assert that their faith is rational while entertaining the possibility that what counts as rational might in some way be inadequate, deficient. The theological task might then be, not to berate reason, but to seek its restoration.

Second, there should be no blanket condemnation of 'the Enlightenment'. The eighteenth century saw advances in social, philosophical and political thought which cannot just be laid aside and which have abiding theological significance. Theological criticism has to be reserved for the extension of a narrow rationalism into areas where it is inadequate. Such a criticism is, of course, not new. Criticisms of the dominance of the 'experimental philosophy' and the 'mechanical philosophy' to the domain of the human spirit were common in the nineteenth century. Third, there should be no more attempts on behalf of theology to discredit science. Science and theology have more in common than ever (Polkinghorne; Peacocke), and Christians do their faith no good by joining in anti-scientific propaganda while enjoying the benefits which science and technology bestow on them. The theological challenge must be reserved for the extension of scientific rationality to all areas of enquiry and dimensions of life, with the result that whatever a science cannot comprehend or validate through investigation can be epistemically discarded, or (what amounts to the same thing) safely confined to the realm of opinion.

Rational faith and real knowledge

Belief in the Resurrection of Jesus is realistic, cognitive and rational. The claim that the belief is realistic is the claim that a phenomenal event, an actual historical occurrence, happened, something which was more than a growing conviction among the disciples that Calvary was not the end. If Jesus did not rise from the dead, then, as Paul said, our faith is futile and we are still in our sins (1 Corinthians 15:17). There is a view that the New Testament accounts of the Resurrection amount to a myth, designed to convey the truth that even though Christ died the death of a common criminal and his mission appeared to have failed, his spirit, his love, his message, and his power to make whole continue to survive because they are of God. This view has much to commend it, not least because it makes sense of Christian experience. But it settles the troublesome historical and philosophical questions in advance by assuming that divine intervention in raising Jesus is inessential to Resurrection faith. It is hardly consistent with what the Church has traditionally taught about the Resurrection (though that may not be a decisive argument against it). And there remains

175

too big a gap between the 'surface grammar' of Resurrection, that God raised Jesus, and the 'depth grammar', that God's power to save, revealed in Jesus, still goes on. Realism insists that the raising of Jesus is not merely experience-dependent. But realism is not literalism (yet another lurking post-enlightenment assumption: for the best treatment of theological realism, see Soskice, chapters 6–8). The claim of realism is that something happened at Easter: how it happened, not even the scriptures tell us.

The belief that Jesus really did rise is therefore cognitive; faith in the Risen Christ is a *cognitive act.* The force of 'cognitive' is that there is something knowable external to the human mind which, in grasping, the mind 'cognises'. Theologians must not be enticed by the simplistic distinctions between facts and values or events and interpretations. MacIntyre convincingly shows that 'facts, like telescopes and wigs for gentlemen, were a seventeenth-century invention' (MacIntyre (2), p. 357: see also MacIntyre (1), p. 76). 'Fact', he reminds us, translates *factum,* 'something done', and is therefore inseparable from purpose. Once the Resurrection is construed as a possible but highly problematical 'fact' ripped away from the settled concepts that give it its meaning, or alternatively, as some dubious event the likelihood of whose occurrence is wrenched from the interpretation which links it to God's deed and our salvation, then it becomes the prisoner of a discourse which inevitably eclipses its meaning.

A faith in God who has a real existence independent of our minds is a cognitive faith; a faith in God who is our 'ultimate concern' may not be. A faith in Christ crucified and risen is cognitive if it has as its object Christ crucified and risen; a faith in Christ who is only alive in our hearts or who makes us feel 'free' (van Buren, p. 134) may not be cognitive at all. A cognitive act is one that reaches out towards something known and is distinguishable from volition (an act of will) and emotion. An act of faith (see below) is one which does involve will and emotion, but there is a cognitive element in it which cannot be collapsed into volition or feeling. If there was not a real Resurrection, independently of our recognition of it, then Christ is not living in our hearts. A real Resurrection is a precondition of cognitive faith.

The belief that Jesus rose from the dead is rational. By 'rational' let us stipulate that it must be consistent with our other beliefs, including our strong belief that normally dead people do not rise. It must be coherent. It must be consistent with all the available evidence. It must express a personal judgement, in other words, a judgement which is an act of the whole person. And, since all rationalities are 'tradition-constituted' (MacIntyre (2), ch. 18) it must belong to a tradition, in this case the broad spectrum of Christian traditions which affirm that Christ is risen.

Actions, reasons and causes

For there to be knowledge there must be at least a knower and something known. In the case of the Resurrection the something known is an action, the action of God in raising Jesus as well as a person, Jesus, who was raised. It is important to point this out, not least because the understanding of action is a whole branch of philosophy and some categories borrowed from the philosophy of action can help. Looking at what is involved in a human action might help in understanding the action of God in raising Jesus.

An event in the physical world is an action if it is brought about purposively by a human being or agent. An action therefore presupposes an agent who is free, who has a reason for acting or intention (the two are not the same), and who can and does perform the action. An agent has a first-person perspective on his or her action. An observer has a third-person perspective on the agent's action. So, in running down the street only I know whether I am trying to catch the bus, pursuing a thief, being pursued by a thief or having a jog. An observer on observing my purposive behaviour can interpret it, albeit without difficulty. There are two features of actions which are of particular help in understanding the action of God in raising Jesus, one about causality, the other about interpretation.

177

ADRIAN THATCHER

Suppose I was jogging, and doing so because I believed that I needed to be fitter. I had just seen a programme on personal fitness and decided that I would take more exercise. Was the programme the cause of my jogging? Clearly not, since if an event is an action at all it has to be chosen freely, and if I am caused to act then I am not acting but responding. But let us say the programme made a big impact on me. It was a factor. In that case, my beliefs that I am not fit but ought to be do contribute to my actions. But neuroscience cannot cope with beliefs as causes (Davidson). Actions cannot be constrained by causal explanations. There are two reasons for this. First, whatever parts of my brain are working when I get dressed for jogging and go, they accompany my intention and are not identical with it. Second, there are at least two types of explanation required in the case of human actions. These are causal, and personal (Swinburne).

When God raised Jesus, a divine agent was acting. Now, if in the human case action is finally unamenable to causal explanation, it is not too difficult to expect that in the divine case causal explanation may not get very far either. That is, the questions, 'How did God raise Jesus?', 'How did God transform Christ's body into his glorified body?', 'How did God violate nature's laws?' are pertinent but unproductive because when God acts he is under no obligation to act in accordance with what we understand about causality. And it turns out that what we know about causality is of little use to us because, when we want to explain our own actions, causal explanations do not and cannot suffice. We need reasons.

When God raised Jesus he had good reasons for doing so. Of course, only God knows what they are, but scripture and theology provide convincing suggestions (which are also personal explanations) of why this unique event occurred. God wanted to vindicate his Son Jesus, to share his Son's risen life with us, to give us victory over death, and so on. The 'why?' questions, not the 'how?' questions, are the important ones. If we are to understand what happened at Easter it is reasons we need to go for; the purposes of

178

God have to be consulted and personal explanations found. When someone goes jogging down the street at least it is clear to an observer that he or she is doing so. When God raised Jesus it was not clear at all what God was doing. Not only was no observer there, no one is accustomed to meeting people who have risen from the dead; nor do we know what to expect of resurrected bodies. If we had a bank of experiences of or with resurrected persons we could produce profiles of what they are like – whether they need sustenance, how free their movements are, whether they could have children, whether they show signs of ageing, whether they have total recall of their previous lives, and so on. Such profiles are, of course, absurd (and perhaps irreverent), yet they are just the sort of things that empirical investigations come up with. However important it is to investigate exhaustively what might have happened at the Resurrection, it is important to admit the limitations of such a study. What happened cannot in the last resort be open to empirical description.

Is the Resurrection, then, believable? Yes, it is, and the rest of this essay will be devoted to outlining how the human mind, operating with a broader conception of what is to count as cognition, is able to affirm the Resurrection. It has already been argued that a cognitive act has real objects of knowledge. Let us now examine some of the different elements which together comprise a cognitive act. This might be called the anatomy of cognition.

Faith

So, first, there is an element of faith involved in every act of cognition, irrespective of the nature of the object. When the object of our cognition is the Risen Christ the element of faith is pronounced. Here we might contrast 'faith seeking understanding' with 'reason seeking evidence'. The first approach is initially prepared to suspend disbelief (in the search for knowledge); the second is initially prepared to suspend belief (in the search for proof). Michael Polanyi has done much to restore the element of faith to cognition.

179

He speaks of 'the fiduciary rootedness of all rationality' (Polanyi, pp. 296–7). In a section called 'The Critique of Doubt' he wanted 'to face the fact that every perception of things, particularly by our eyes, involves implications about the nature of things which could be false'. Our perceptions of colours, sizes, distances and shapes, he continues, are 'determined by our innate physiological inclinations and their subsequent development under the influence of our experience'.

The import of Polanyi's critique of Cartesian doubt as a search for certainty is the destruction of the myth of 'virgin minds' seeking 'virgin data', unspoiled by subjective interpretation. The myth is replaced by personal participation in the objects of investigation, active involvement in what is studied, faith in the knowability of the world and the capability of the human mind, through 'personal knowledge' to know it. Polanyi does not have in mind the Resurrection of Christ at all here, but his insights into perception are valuable none the less, for the Resurrection was an event within history, within the phenomenal world, and video cameras installed in the tomb would have recorded something, even if that something was no more than a surplus of light on the cassette. The accounts the Gospels give us of the Resurrection are tantalising for what they do not reveal. Between them they do not claim a single eyewitness. But what one rationality might reject as an implausible candidate for serious belief, the other might be drawn to as potentially a series of unique and miraculous events which demand meticulous investigation. And among the 'phenomena' that would require investigation would be the claims Jesus made for himself, what sense the Resurrection would make, if it occurred, of the purposes of God, the experience of the disciples, expectations of the end of the age, and so on.

Conation

A third element in an act of cognition may be a conative one. The term is sometimes used in the philosophy of art (by Reid, for example). The conative element of knowledge is the attempt or striving to see significance in an object of contemplation or attention. The mind is not separated from the will in conation. Whenever this separation occurs it is too easy to end up believing anything and everything we want to, irrespective of its truth. Suppose I am confronted by a Picasso, or I cannot escape a piece of the music of Messiaen. When confronted with the unfamiliar I dislike being reminded of my ignorance and want to pass on. And it is easier to do so. But I suspend my inclinations. I attempt, scepticism suspended, to let the unfamiliar 'get to me'. This can only happen if I am prepared to be receptive. In the attempt to see new depths and images in painting and colours in music I am being conative. I may see them: and I may not. Success cannot be guaranteed. So it is with the Gospel story and its marvellous climax. The analogy between aesthetic and religious knowing does not break down just because the success of the cognitive act cannot be guaranteed in advance. Preachers of the gospel ask only that their hearers open themselves to the possibility that the gospel might be true. It is through the attempt to understand what is encountered that what is encountered lets itself be understood.

Envisionment

A third element in cognition may be envisionment. Envisionment is conceptually related to imagination, and imagination has a philosophical history which in the modern period begins with Hume and Kant, is adopted by Coleridge and Schelling and in this century notably by Sartre (Warnock). The notion is contested, but that must not make us fearful of its theological application. One recent writer speaks of how 'the exercise of imagination moves us away from the conventional, the common, and the familiar'. Imagination, she says,

> is what allows us to envision possibilities in or beyond the actualities in which we are immersed. We do not thus merely escape in thought the bounds of reality; we know that something other

181

> than this immediate temporary reality is possible – and we may
> then be excited to effect changes in the world. (Hanson, p. 138)

The fertile imagination can envision new possibilities within what is humdrum and familiar. True, a fertile imagination can also entertain perverted fantasies and dream up great evils (as the romantics also discovered), but in science and art alike it is also a powerful means of discovery.

Faced with the Resurrection narratives their initial implausibility is undeniably high, for everyone knows that dead people do not come back from death. But the world where people do not come back from death constitutes 'the actualities in which we are immersed' and leads to the formulation of the question whether there is any hope for us beyond. What is encountered in the proclamation of the Risen Christ 'moves us away from the conventional, the common, and the familiar'. But implausibility could perhaps be the key to the recognition of God's action, since there is no human constraint on what God might do, and what is doubtless implausible historically and biologically (dead people remain dead) may be utterly plausible if viewed in the light of God's self-giving love, his identification with us in finitude and suffering. Envisionment enables initial scepticism to be suspended, not for ever, but for long enough for the mystery to be probed and the imagination to be grasped.

Insight

A fourth element in the act of cognition is insight. Bernard Lonergan began his magisterial work on insight with the simple illustration of a detective story. Readers in the dark at the end of a whodunit may remain ignorant of the identity of the murderer because 'reaching the solution is not the mere apprehension of any clue, not the mere memory of all, but a quite distinct activity of organising intelligence that places the full set of clues in a unique explanatory perspective' (Lonergan, p. x). That is insight, and it consists not of an isolated act of knowledge but an ability to under-

stand all that is known about something in a new way, a way
in which the whole becomes credible, and makes sense.

One might surmise that Mark 16:1–8 could have been
written in just such a way as to evoke the very insight from
the reader that gives it sense. We are left with no one
among the faithful expecting what is to happen, least of all
the women who go to anoint the body, worrying about rolling away the stone of the tomb. Already a 'tale of the
unexpected' is beginning to unfold. An anonymous young
man tells them he is risen – why should they believe him?
The reader is left not knowing whether the women see Jesus
in Galilee as the young man forecast: the narrative ends
with the women silent and fearful. But that is not quite all:
'trembling and astonishment had come upon them' (v. 8).
None of the details given in the narrative provide answers
to the questions put by modernity. But we can imagine what
the women may already be envisioning – the unexpected
has already gripped their minds and they know they are
caught up in a miraculous act of God. We too can respond
to the same story. The human understanding arrives at the
Resurrection by means of insight. Insight is that way of
seeing which gives the 'unique explanatory perspective' on
Jesus and on the purpose of God for humankind and for
history.

Contemplation

A fifth element in the cognitive act is contemplative. 'Contemplative knowledge' is a term which may be contrasted
with Tillich's account of 'controlling knowledge'. With controlling knowledge, the knower dominates what he or she
knows and manipulates and utilises it for his or her own
purposes. It represents the triumph of technical rationality
over its objects. 'Controlling knowledge looks upon its object
as something which cannot return its look' (Tillich,
pp. 108–9). With contemplative knowledge the knower con-
templates but does not control; he or she stands at the
boundary between knowledge and what is beyond knowledge. In contemplation one knows that one does not know.

183

One gains a sensitivity to mystery and a positive appreciation of it. This appreciation of the limits to knowledge reflects back on the enquiring mind, giving it a permanent reminder of the need for cognitive humility.

Much has been written lately about sensitivity to mystery. Harold Schilling wrote of this as an essential element of the scientific outlook in the apprehension of both the micro- and macroworlds. Both are unimaginable to scientists living at the beginning of the present century. The facility to be surprised, to expect to be wrong, to be baffled, in short to be overwhelmed by the sheer immensity of what has been discovered and what is still there to discover, is an attitude which is continually necessary when complex investigation is to be carried out. But the sense of mystery which is part of the epistemic appreciation of the physical world is not far from what Christians have themselves experienced when they have spoken of Christ as God's mystery, disclosing to them what they did not expect to receive but which, when they are open to it, has the force of revelation.

Feeling

The act of faith is a holistic act of the person. God addresses us as persons; our salvation is for all aspects of our being, and in worship we are involved as the totalities we are. Whenever persons are understood as 'wholes' a serious problem arises about identifying which parts the 'whole' comprises. This problem cannot be addressed now. Let us stipulate that people are totalities involving mind, will, and feeling. The Resurrection was a real historical event: a judgement has to be made that it happened, and this judgement is made, we might say, by the mind. But the mind making the judgement is the mind of a person, and persons are clearly influenced by the will (the conative element) and by feeling. Let us say, then, that sixthly, feeling is an undeniable and essential element in moral and aesthetic knowledge and it is an element in our knowledge of the raising of Jesus. Through it we are able to appropriate that we are the dear

184

objects of God's love for whose sakes Jesus died and rose again.

These elements of the cognitive act represent an attempt to show how, with an enlarged range of what is to count as cognitive, the act of faith in the Risen Christ is rational. The elements do, of course, overlap, and the list is incomplete. The Resurrection of Jesus cannot be demonstrated to have happened. MacIntrye has written of 'competing rationalities', describing the inability to choose between them as the fundamental crisis facing post-enlightenment people (MacIntyre (2), ch. 1). He speaks of 'that type of rationality which is presupposed by tradition-constituted enquiry' (p. 390). There is no single way of determining what rationality is and so of what can count as a rational act. But there is a type of rationality which embraces Resurrection faith and belongs to a tradition which has the Risen Christ as its living source. This tradition will not be shaken by narrow dogmas about what is to be believed.

I am grateful to my friends Liz Stuart and Paul Grosch at the College of St Mark and St John, Plymouth, for their helpful and constructive comments on an earlier version of this essay.

Bibliography

Ayer, A.J., *Language, Truth and Logic* (London: Gollancz, 18th imp., 1970)

Bentham, J., *Introduction to the Principles of Morals and Legislation* (1780), ch. 1

Coley, N.G. and Hall, V.M.D., *Darwin to Einstein: Primary Sources on Science and Belief* (Harlow: Longman, 1980)

Davidson, D., 'Psychology as Philosophy', in J. Glover (ed.), *The Philosophy of Mind* (Oxford: Oxford University Press, 1976)

Descartes, R., *The Meditations*, in *Discourse on Method and Other Writings* (Harmondsworth: Penguin, 1968)

Gunton, C., *Enlightenment and Alienation* (Grand Rapids, Mich.: Eerdmans, 1985), especially part 1

Hanson, K., 'Prospects for the Good Life: Education and Perceptive Imagination', in K. Egan and D. Nadaner (eds), *Imagination and Education* (Milton Keynes: Open University Press, 1988)

Hartley, D., *Observations on Man* (1769), chs 1, 2.

Hume, D., *Enquiries concerning Human Understanding and concerning the*

185

Principles of Morals (1777) (Oxford: Oxford University Press, 3rd edn 1975), section 10

Kung, H.,*Does God Exist?* (London: Collins, Fount Paperbacks, 1984), section A

Lonergan, B., *Insight* (London: Darton, Longman & Todd, 1958)

MacIntyre, A. (1), *After Virtue* (London: Duckworth, 2nd imp., 1982)

MacIntyre, A. (2), *Whose Justice? Which Rationality?* (London: Duckworth, 1988)

Mill, J.S., *Utilitarianism* (1863), chs 1, 2.

Newbigin, L., *The Other Side of 1984* (Geneva: World Council of Churches, 1983)

Peacocke, A., *Creation and the World of Science* (Oxford: Clarendon Press, 1979)

Polkinghorne, J., *One World: The Interaction of Science and Theology* (London: SPCK, 1986)

Polanyi, M., *Personal Knowledge* (London: Routledge & Kegan Paul, 1958)

Reid, L.A., 'Cognitive Feeling', *Journal of the Philosophy of Education*, xiv, 1, 1981)

Schilling, H., *The New Consciousness in Science and Religion* (London: SCM, 1973)

Soskice, J.M., *Metaphor and Religious Language* (Oxford: Clarendon Press, 1985)

Swinburne, R., *The Existence of God* (Oxford: Clarendon Press, 1979), ch. 7

Thatcher, A., 'The Recovery of Christian Education', in L. Francis and A. Thatcher (eds), *Christian Perspectives for Education* (Leominster: Fowler Wright, 1990)

Tillich, P., *Systematic Theology* 1 (London: Nisbet, 1953)

van Buren, P., *The Secular Meaning of the Gospel* (London: SCM, 1963)

Warnock, M., *Imagination* (London: Faber & Faber, 1976)